Dia
DEVONSHIRE
WALKER

was conceived and written by
CHIPS BARBER

who was ably assisted by
SALLY BARBER

Another "monumental" production from . . . . .

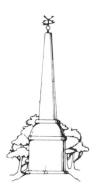

OBELISK PUBLICATIONS

Also by the Author (and his wife):
Around & About the Haldon Hills
The Lost City of Exeter
Diary of a Dartmoor Walker
The Torbay Book

PLATE ACKNOWLEDGEMENTS
Jane Reynolds for all drawings
Dave Whalley for all maps
Tom Bolt for Princetown Prison
R W J Norton for Meldon and ponies
Nicholas Toyne (Jerome Dessain) for the Goats' Walk
All other photographs by Chips Barber
Les Ford for black & white processing

Front Cover: Snow scene near Hound Tor (Chips Barber)
Back Cover: 'Waterfall' on the East Dart River (Stephen Ayres)
Page 3: Marsh Falls on the East Dart River
Page 4: The Teign Gorge below Castle Drogo
Page 6: Bell Tor and Chinkwell Tor
Page 8: River Teign near Fingle Bridge

First published in 1986
by Obelisk Publications
2 Church Hill, Pinhoe, Exeter.
Designed, typeset and printed in Great Britain by
Penwell Ltd, Parkwood, Callington, Cornwall.

'Whilst every care has been taken,
the author cannot accept responsibility
for any inaccuracies'   ·

ISBN 0 946651 00 0

CONTENTS

Introduction

The windswept, boulder-strewn landscape of Dartmoor and the wild, almost unspoilt coastline of South Devon provides the perfect stage for the majority of the explorations included in this book. Written in the same vein as "Diary of a Dartmoor Walker", this edition adds some different areas, like the Tamar Valley and the Haldon Hills, to give fresh ideas to any rambler looking for new territories and wider horizons.

"Diary of a Devonshire Walker" is an extremely lighthearted look at the best of the Devonshire countryside, as seen through the eyes of a non-conformist Dartmoor walking guide.

The seventeen walks are all fully illustrated, although it must be admitted that at times the conditions were too poor for photography and I had to go back and do re-takes.

The book is dedicated to all those fortunate people who have traversed the moors with me on fine days and also to all those unfortunate folk who have struggled against wind, rain, sleet, snow and sheer bad leadership in more inclement times. Many of them are featured in this volume, whilst all the others will have to be patient and wait for the next edition in a few years time.

I would like to extend an open invitation to anyone who would like to join us on future rambles. But remember, if any unusual, or mildly amusing, incidents occur, they will be taken down and may be used in evidence!

Happy rambling!

Chips Barber

1
Dartmoor—The 'In' Continent

One of the most appreciated walks in "Diary of a Dartmoor Walker" was the one which was called 'The Belstone Renard'. This was sub-titled 'Froggies in the Boggies' on account of the trials and tribulations experienced in taking foreign students, of French extraction, on a watery circuit of Northern Dartmoor. I never imagined that a more extraordinary minority group would present themselves for a moorland jaunt but, sure enough, the staff of an Incontinence Clinic requested just such an excursion.

The fun started well in advance of the event. When I asked them when they wanted to walk, they politely replied, "At your own convenience".

The appointed day arrived early in March, and the timing couldn't have been more perfect; the previous week's blizzards had blown themselves out, the air was still and the cloudless skies were deep blue. The moor was carpeted in a layer of snow which was a foot deep in places—a scene of unparalleled beauty illuminated by brilliant sunshine.

In the lower car park at Haytor we were warned, in dire tones, by a man clearing away the snow drifts, that we would need several spades and a good deal of toil if we were ever to get our minibus out of its spot in the car park on our return—"*If* you return!" Personally, I found it hard to believe that such a situation might arise as, although it was early in the morning, the temperature must have been at least 10 degrees centigrade and a thaw had already begun.

Nevertheless, we respected the advice of the good man and cautiously set off towards the old granite quarries beneath Haytor. The going was hard, but soft, if you see what I mean! Inside the quarry it was even warmer and many of the protective garments and thermal undies donned ten minutes earlier were re-packed within their various rucksacks.

Although many of the party could not see the Haytor Granite Tramway, despite the fact that we were walking along it, they were still keen to learn a little of its history. It was Devon's first railway and opened in 1820. Its rails were made of the same material that it was constructed to carry, granite. The route, from the many

9

An icy view of the Haytor Loo!

quarries in and around Haytor, led for about 8 miles around the hillsides, ever descending into the Bovey Basin at Teigngrace. Here it linked with the Stover Canal, a 2 miles long watercourse, which in turn led to the Teign Estuary and beyond to Teignmouth. Here the granite was transhipped to larger vessels which carried the granites off to be used in many notable buildings, ranging from Nelson's Column to London Bridge.

The railway's opening ceremony was a colourful pageant with a British Ensign flag flying proudly from Haytor's summit. Evidently there was a number of beautiful ladies present: "Never," wrote an ecstatic newspaper reporter, "was Haytor's sod graced with such blooming fair ones!" There was dancing and merriment (naturally, with so much 'talent' around) and much excitement.

However, despite the promising start, poor management and the competition of more easily obtainable Cornish granite meant that the undertaking never reached its economic potential and, after sporadic working, the last granites were hewn about 1858.

Haytor Down and Black Hill were next on our agenda and

The struggle away from Haytor and its quarries

appeared no problem as the gradients ahead were of a gentle nature and the surface vegetation was not too strewn with clitter. Reality though was another matter. The undulating, rippled surface had been disguised by a carpet of snow as smooth as the surface of a snooker table. So, at each pace forward, your foot would either penetrate a mere six inches, or your leg would suddenly disappear until terra firma was reached. It was certainly a case of "the firma the ground, the less the terra"! The net result of this uncertain means of travel was that we all kept keeling over every few steps. Fortunately the cushion afforded by the snow meant that no injuries were sustained and great hilarity ensued. It took an age to cross this snow field until, nearer the cairn on Black Hill, less farcical conditions prevailed.

Photographically the moor looked superb—the outlines of tors protruding with uncanny definition. However we also wanted to see what the woodlands looked like in snow so we drifted off the lofty Black Hill and descended, like winter skiers, down over Trendlebere Down into the valley of the Becka Brook. A lot of slushy surface mud was ample evidence that the valley floor was a sun trap, and the romantic notion of icicles dangling off snow swept trees was soon dispelled.

We crossed a small bridge over the Becka Brook and followed the tortuously steep, and oft-times slippery, path towards Becka Falls.

For once everything was all white on Black Hill

Today, the spectacle of the waterfall was an attractive rather than a breathtaking one. However, we didn't linger because we had an appointment to keep with the MCC.

Back on a higher elevation, on the alps of Dartmoor, snow again lay thick and held a peculiar fascination (which is hard to explain as, for the majority of the time, it is contemptible stuff). The Kestor Inn was like a winter ski resort lodge. Plenty of folk had ventured out and the air was so stale within the inn, in comparison to the pure air without, that we opted to dine outside. Snow was swept from the seats and tables and there was no hint of regret or cold as the conversation flowed. Whilst we ate, the subject of work was taboo!

The good life had to end and, happily satiated, we left this cricketing pub behind and eschewed the long climb up and over Hayne Down. Around the arc of the moorland fringe, great clouds threw themselves up into wonderful shapes like towering mountain ranges. But, above our heads, it was as deep blue as the South Pacific Sea and, beneath our feet, as white as only virgin snow glistening bright could be.

I missed a rare opportunity at Swallerton Gate. A lady of great age stood at her cottage door and gave us a friendly greeting. This was originally The Hound Tor Inn and I would have loved to learn more from her about the times when it was a thriving alehouse. But, such is the debilitating nature of alcohol, combined with glorious scenery, I was thoroughly distracted from furthering my Dartmoor education.

Hound Tor was a scene of winter skiing. Makeshift sleds and toboggans weaved around us as we attempted to reach the tor's summit. At this point, several members suddenly exhibited a strong urge to make a snowball of world beating proportions. In no time at all a colossal spherical object of awesome dimensions was being rolled down the hillside towards Hound Tor's medieval village. Had the gradient been a bit sharper there might well have been an archaeological disaster! Fortunately the snowball disintegrated well short of this target and we slithered our way past the historic settlement.

Snowy Hound Tor

That great Dartmoor writer, William Crossing, (known affectionately by our group as, "dear old WC") tells a story of Grea Tor rocks which indeed is a sad tale. In his epic guide he relates a tale of long ago when a young courting couple regularly visited this tor. Alas, the poor young man went to war and never returned. His beloved died of a broken heart and was laid to rest at nearby Manaton churchyard, thus leaving the rock all alone. I rather gained the impression that "WC" felt more sorry for the rock than the couple!

The sun was low in the sky as we skirted Grea Tor Rocks on the track down and over the Becka Brook. The last real climb of the day was to reach Smallacombe Rocks. The evening's icy chill was enough to hasten our footsteps across the open moor, and back

13

There's no business like snow business! Haytor and Rippon Tor beyond

beyond the quarries below Haytor. There had been quite a thaw and the old tramway was clearly discernible. Our attention was drawn to the twinkling of lights in distant lands. Clusters of them indicated the many small villages and large towns of South Devon. Bovey, Chudleigh, Newton, Torquay, Brixham and Marldon all shone bright—the numbers of glows clearly proportional to the size of each settlement. And there were odd lights, like that of Berry Head which flashed its characteristic beam from afar, that accompanied us in to the end of a dramatic and memorable walk.

Incidentally, if you are wondering about the reference to the MCC at the Kestor Inn, I should explain that the pub sign proclaims that this is the headquarters of the Manaton Cricket Club!

2

Around Berry Head on a One Way Ticket

I really must learn to be more cautious when discovering that some of my friends are members of the Long Distance Walking Association and they suggest a pleasant stroll together. Inevitably it will mean being lured into a walk of great length, with them disappearing over the horizon with consummate ease, and me being left on the lower slopes of despair . . . My two colleagues, Terry and Dennis, may not look like Superman but both could certainly

outwalk him! Just such an occasion arose not too long ago and the memory of that painful pilgrimage will long remain.

The walk started easily enough—on a steam train! The plan was simple. We would catch the Torbay and Dartmouth Railway from Paignton to Kingswear, and then walk back around the coastline.

The dictates and limitations of the Steam Railway's timetable meant that our stroll began at a much later hour than usual. However, as it was high summer, and light until late, this didn't bother us. We emerged at Kingswear amidst hundreds of tourists who were all set to explore Dartmouth. Within minutes of leaving the station we had left everybody else behind. We climbed the steep Alma Steps and headed out of Kingswear along Beacon Road to a track leading through National Trust land.

By now we were high above the mouth of the Dart, a scene of both great activity and beauty. Dartmouth's medieval castle (1481) stood sentinel at the gate to this deep water haven. Beneath us was its twin counterpart on the Kingswear side, fortress home of a local Member of Parliament.

By the time we had travelled the one and a half miles to Brownstone Farm I had realised that my companions were no ordinary ramblers. Whilst I made a strenuous effort to notch about four miles per hour, they did it with little effort. They had a rhythm to their stride and movement that I sadly lacked. Only with odd spurts of running did I manage to keep up with them.

The National Trust have acquired a considerable amount of coastline in these parts in recent years. We headed beyond Coleton and decided to savour some of the delights of what was previously privately owned territory. Therefore after pleasant, greatly undulating countryside we reached the coast near Ivy Cove.

I was about to pause, and change lenses on my camera, in order to take some shots of the abundant sea birds, when I realised that my partners were almost out of sight. This was particularly disconcerting because, instead of a gently sloping path, the way ahead was like a vertical, many humped big dipper. They just kept marching on, in the same gear and at the same speed.

Now, I admit I enjoyed the challenge yielded all the way along the coast, but I must confess I was dismayed at the climb out of Scabbacombe Sands and was thoroughly incredulous at the never ending, near vertical rise up from Man Sands! The one compensation was that, in the whole of this section, despite it being high summer, we did not pass another single person the entire way. Scabbacombe and Man Sands must surely be two of the quietest beaches in Devon.

Sharkham Point marks the boundary between the end of a wild, untamed and remote coastline and the beginning of the most concentrated tourist area in South West England. In the past Sharkham possessed several iron ore mines and pits and, if you look closely, you can see several remains and scars. However, I was so determined not to get further behind that I didn't even see Sharkham Point, leave alone the mine workings!

It was of some relief to me that the path over Durl Head and along to Berry Head was not as alpine as it had been earlier. I noted that one of the Holiday Camps bordering the cliff top had gone to great lengths to create an extravaganza of exotic vegetation with many sub-tropical plants, bushes and trees, providing an excellent wind break and visual amenity.

To say that we took a late lunch is an understatement as it was about 3.30 pm when we eventually ground to a halt by the small lighthouse on Berry Head. At last I felt on familiar territory, as I

Berry Head Lighthouse - taken without a flash!

had researched all around this area for "The Torbay Book". As we try to avoid repetition, avoid repetition, I will not tell you all the wondrous tales concerning this great limestone bastion. For a modest outlay you can acquire these treasures of local interest for yourself!

The Long Distance Walker must have a short distance digestive system! No sooner had the last sandwich gone, than we were off again at a steady, monotonous four miles per hour. We passed the Berry Head House Hotel and headed around Brixham's harbour side with such pace that the slowly drifting, seething mass of holidaymakers were obliged to move aside to let our three man express train belt through.

Although Churston Cove looked inviting with its translucent deep blue waters, there was no time for fun as this was a walk! The climb up out of this cove was a drain on the already depleted energy reserves.

From above Churston Cove the path to Elbury is extremely easy and gentle on the legs. Unfortunately, dense woods on the seaward side, and a high fence on the landward side, reduced views to a minimum. In a short time we were at Elbury Cove, a favourite haunt for beach parties. At regular intervals, along the high tide line, we spied the tell-tale signs of rings of stones used for barbeque fires.

The next half mile was bliss. The low cliffs of Galmpton Point, or Honeycombe Rocks, proved no problem and we again joined the crowds at Broadsands Beach. The coastline we had just traversed was formerly owned by Lord Churston and, in the past, it was necessary to obtain written permission to walk it. In those days Broadsands was a shallow lagoon which eventually silted up to become a swamp. The local authority drained it, reclaimed it, and it is now a most popular rendezvous for beach devotees.

We were now on the last stretch and, although the coastline had been invaded by housing, the views around Tor Bay provided adequate compensation. The coastal path still rises and falls, but great flights of steps past Waterside Camp, and on into Goodrington, enabled us to negotiate these steep gradients. At one point the others again got ahead of me so I had to run to catch up. One resident, clearing his garden which abutted on the path, called out, "Why are you running?" Even though I am normally a very

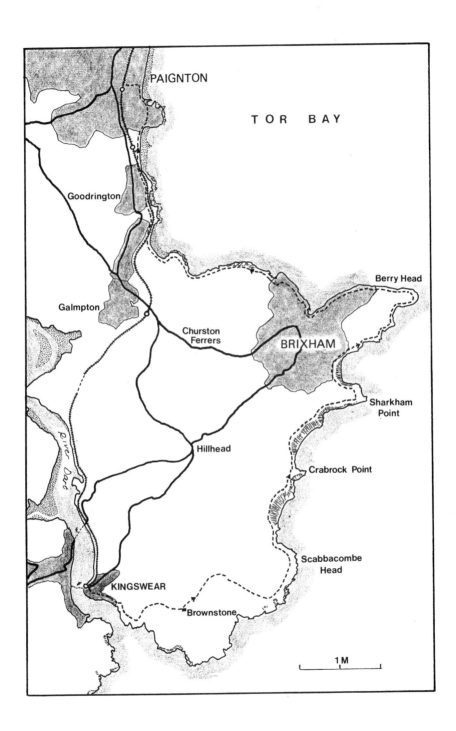

PAIGNTON

T O R   B A Y

Goodrington

Galmpton

Churston
Ferrers

BRIXHAM

Berry Head

Sharkham
Point

Hillhead

Crabrock Point

River Dart

Scabbacombe
Head

KINGSWEAR

Brownstone

1 M

sociable person, on this occasion I just could not manage to summon up enough breath to acknowledge this polite enquiry. I hope he reads this book and then perhaps he might understand and even sympathise.

The final confirmation of Dennis and Terry's superior fitness came at Roundham Head when they opted to traverse the perimeter of the headland. Meanwhile I took a short cut and strolled along the street to Paignton Harbour, and a welcome rest. When they arrived, I had just enough energy, and cheek, to greet them with, "What kept you lads, then?"

3
Forty-Five Maidens from Maidencombe and a few Bachelors as well

Presumably as a result of a regular 'walking' spot on local radio, I occasionally get requests to put my feet where my mouth is and lead a stroll. A typical occasion occurred on one of those long summer evenings of burnished gold, when the sun reluctantly sinks after hanging around in the sky just long enough to entice a faithful band of followers to dabble in fun, frustration and folly.

The Goats' Walk - 'kids' stuff!

What a sight to behold—45 'assorted' ladies alighting from their coach! What a sight to behold when 45 'assorted' ladies all start following the only man! Fortunately I took my wife with me as chaperone!

We left our conveyance, appropriately, at Maidencombe, half way between Torquay and Teignmouth. And so it was that the throng of maidens entered the valley of maidens. They followed enthusiastically, but so painfully slowly, on the hill back out of Maidencombe towards Watcombe. There was certainly a dire struggle between the steepness of the coastal path and their metabolism. The topography won.

Those stalwarts at the front of the Alphington Wives Group waited patiently on the Goats Path whilst I briefed them on the significance of the path's name and told them how, in days of old, that is up to 1902, goats were a common sight along here. Sadly most of the goats gorged themselves to death. A similar thought occurred to me about the back markers of our group as they consumed various edibles along the way, but I kept this thought to myself, after all, they had to keep their energy levels up!

We entered the gloomy shade of the "Valley of Rocks", a delightful woodland retreat. Although I related quite a lot of historical digest about Watcombe, notably its claim to launching the British film industry in the early 1920s, the fact that caused most amusement was the reputed popularity of Watcombe beach for gay individuals.

After that discourse the back markers caught up, slightly hot and bothered, uttering polysyllabic unutterables about the gross undulation of the terrain. To add insult to injury, blisters and breathlessness, the hill towards Petit Tor provided an even longer and more difficult climb. Actually there are many benches along this stretch, which may have provided respite, but these were either vandalised or in such a state that sitting on them would have constituted a major health hazard!

Inevitably those with the scarlet complexions, and the steam coming out of the ears, found it an impossible chore. By mutual agreement we decided to terminate their misery and allowed them to seek the sanctuary of St Marychurch, just along the road from Petitor Point—glistening in the warmth of a gorgeous summer evening. How inviting the diminutive Cary Arms appeared down at Babbacombe jetty, hundreds of feet below. I would have happily run down there, downed a few pints and run back up again! However, the very thought of another climb was far too much for these good ladies and so we followed the coast path around to Babbacombe's Model Village.

The ladies all sighed with relief at the sight of the coaches standing in the adjacent car park. I felt quite choked to have to

Into the valley . . .

Petit Tor - a tor many miles from Dartmoor

inform them that none of these were our own bus and that we had another mile to go. But at least the last mile would be flat (apart from the ups and downs).

The geriatric masses ensconced in deck chairs watched us cross Babbacombe Downs. They were obviously bemused at the spectacle of one man leading a long crocodile of ladies.

Here the Babbacombe Theatre provided some entertainment, albeit unintentional. My wife commented that the Bachelors were appearing there for a short summer season. Almost instantaneously I noticed one of them, just a short distance away, in the car park and then I spotted the second one. Now, I ask you, what more could 45 red blooded females want than two of Britain's most famous bachelors? With a frantic scrummaging through pockets, rucksacks or handbags, scraps of paper and writing implements were hurriedly produced. A casual and slightly bemused glance in our direction turned to stunned fascination and there they stood, temporarily rooted to the spot, as first one, then another, of the ladies escaped from the folds of the pack and bore down on them. With persistent cries of, "You are him, aren't you?" the scraps of paper were shoved under their noses. Hastily scribbling a quick autograph, they visibly backed off and wisely disappeared before the entire tribe followed suit.

Amidst much chatter and great excitement, we crossed Walls Hill, a former nine-hole golf course, and descended the path to the

23

Looking from Petit Tor down to Babbacombe Quay

Palace Hotel. To my great relief, they all showed their appreciation of the beauty of the stroll. However, a decided chill descended over the group when I casually enquired, "Where shall we go next year ladies?" Tact has definitely never been high on my list of social attributes!

4

Walking A Dartmoor Railroad— Or something along those lines

I have definitely noticed a tendency, both amongst friends and mere acquaintances, to assume that, because I have written a number of books, I must be 'rolling in it'. Nothing could be further from the truth! Anyone who has ever met me will know that, when walking, I usually travel in a decidedly dishevelled manner, particularly as my Dartmoor wardrobe has fallen into such a sad state of repair that even the moths prefer to dine elsewhere!

So, I felt it was time to raid the piggy bank and treat myself to a Gortex waterproof, the best of the range. I was determined not to suffer any more soakings, or continue to subject myself to ridicule over my state of dress. There is no point listing the price here because, with inflation and time passing, such a sum would be meaningless. However, you could buy the equivalent of 70 pints of best bitter or at least 20 copies of this book, for the same financial outlay.

It was a late spring day when we alighted from our coach near Shapley Common on the B3212. The conditions were perfect, a howling gale straight into our faces and lashings of rain. The sheer noise of the elements rendered conversation impossible, but I am sure I caught a few 'dry' remarks suggesting that I must have planned it. But I knew it was all harmless banter and they were all only too ready to be thoroughly drenched to the skin.

The squelchy lane to Jay's Grave

In the grey gloom the visibility had been reduced to a matter of yards so, at King Tor, I called everyone around in order to point out all the landmarks that would have been seen, had it not been so foggy.

Apparently the wicked, wet, westerly wind was just too much for some of my companions, so the shelter of the woods above Heathercombe Brake was sought. A curious stone with three engraved fishes caused some conversation. Theories about its origin ranged from high rainfall at this location, to trout farms, to a bronze age fish and chip shop. In reality, Heathercombe Brake has religious connections which accounts for this symbol.

The woodland walk to Natsworthy allowed the rest of the crew to dry out and warm up. The reinstated facility of conversation also enabled morale to rise visibly. It was at this point that I happily justified the cost of my outer garment by proving that I was absolutely bone dry on the inside. I also wished that I was taking commission on the sales were to follow my on-the-spot demonstration!

At Natsworthy we paused, in the lee of a high wall, to consume hot, warming drinks before embarking on the path to Jay's Grave. This lane was so deep in mud that we were obliged to walk on the adjacent banks for long stretches.

This is Jay's Grave - Kitty Jay worked and committed suicide at Canna Farm nearby

Bowerman's Nose and a bit more

The next train standing at Moretonhampstead Station . . .

Jay's Grave is a famous Dartmoor landmark. Most people know the sad story of how Kitty Jay hanged herself after becoming pregnant by a man from a higher social class. As suicides were not buried in consecrated ground her body was interred at the nearest crossroads to her home. As usual, we saw fresh flowers on her grave which are left there regularly.

We crossed the featureless Cripdon Down and visited Bowerman's Nose on the side of Hayne Down. So wild were the elements at this point that we hastily descended into Water. Then we made our way on through the woods, down into the great chasm of Lustleigh Cleave and, as usual, we were bemused by the mile posts which increased in distance as we got nearer to Lustleigh.

Lustleigh is arguably the most beautiful of all the Dartmoor settlements, with its beautiful opulent houses that adorn the steeply wooded hillsides rising from the heart of the village. Also, of course, there is the Cleave Hotel strategically located to delight the throat.

I have a vague recollection that our research at the Cleave Hotel was so fruitful that, when we eventually graduated at closing time,

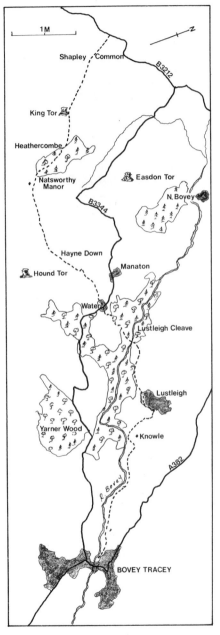

the thick misty rain had gone and left us with quite a decent afternoon for walking.

We had intended following the old Moreton to Bovey branch line for most of the way to Bovey Tracey but, near Lustleigh, it appears to be on private property. Thus we road walked to Rudge and thence south eastwards to Drakeford Bridge. At this point we decided that, as it was the age of the train, we would climb up the old railway bridge and walk along the heavily overgrown track.

A lovely story was related to me about other misusers of the line. At the turn of the century, party-goers from Bovey attending functions at Moretonhampstead were rather restricted by the early return of the last train home. To combat this, it was common for an extra truck to be taken along with the last train up, and this was then shunted into a siding. The party revellers would agree a rendezvous time, in the small hours of the morning, climb aboard this truck, and with a hearty push were sent careering off into the night. As Bovey Tracey is hundreds of feet lower in altitude than Moretonhampstead, gravity motivated the truck into a

A variation on 'an Away Day' - an away night?

good speed on its journey home. It had a manual brake to enable the occupants to control it. The line closed on the 2 March 1959 and it is amazing just how much vegetation has taken root in such a short time.

We followed the line until we reached a small pig farm straddling it and, as pigs are known to be a bit truculent, we left the line near the former site of Hawkmoor Halt rejoining it a few hundred yards further on.

The last section into Bovey is a public right of way. The stony railway track bed was very hard on the feet, but there were no obstacles to avoid and we ended on the right lines!

5
Lydford, the Tavy Cleave and Meldon—
The Land of Thirsty Boots

In the days of my youth, my friends and I had some great walking adventures. Some of them can never be repeated, even though the spark of enthusiasm still burns ever brightly in our hearts and imaginations.

The excitement of each walk always began weeks before the event, in fact, before the dubbin had even dried after the last excursion's mopping up operations! Enormous maps would be spread out, covering great acreages of floor space, so that our cartographic oracle could be fully consulted. In addition to this, bus and train timetables would appear, and the slide-rule technology of route planning thus came into its own. I remember that these planning sessions were just as much fun as the walks themselves, so much so that I still love to play this game today.

Although none of us could drive (we were only about thirteen or fourteen years old at the time), we were spoilt for choice with a tre-

Desolate, derelict and disused - North Tawton Station

mendous network of railway branchlines to choose from—Mr Beeching had not yet wielded his brutal 'axe'. Our only constraints were the idiosyncrasies of the times that trains actually arrived. Even then, delays were fun because more slide rule calculations had to be made so that we were not obliged to spend the night at Lydford or Ivybridge or some other passenger-forsaken station. This is just one of those walks that we did when the locomotives actually stopped at the places where people lived, and provided a service that walkers can now only dream about.

Accompanying me were Bone, Willy, Fingers, Clive, Mike, Jethro, Runciman and Melhuish; together we made a formidable bunch called ESHT, The Episcopal School Hiking Team, whose objective was to get out and enjoy Dartmoor as often as possible.

This assembly met one May morning in 1962 at St David's Station, Exeter with the intention of exploring the north western corner of Dartmoor. As usual, all the others were immaculately equipped whilst I appeared sadly dishevelled and ill prepared. Even my TUF walking boots were secondhand, or should I say second feet? They were in such a state that it was possible, with a wiggle of the toes, to raise the toe cap of the right boot inches from the ground whilst the sole remained on the ground. When walking through pools of water this gave the comical appearance of my right foot thirstily drinking as I progressed!

That train journey to the moor will long remain in my memory. The country stations along the mid-Devon plain, dwarfed by the ever-nearing high Northern Moors, gave way to the moorland fringe, an elevated view of the patchwork quilt of fields stretching away northwards to far off Exmoor. Once Okehampton had been passed there was great expectation and excitement, but always regret at having to leave the train as it travelled onwards towards Tavistock. This town had two railway lines and two stations. On Goose Fair days it was always fun to watch the flotillas of drunken sailors trying to embark on the train to get back to base at Plymouth. Inevitably many a sailor's navigational skills failed him when most needed, and he reached Exeter before the realisation of being all at sea on land set in!

Fortunately it was rare for us to suffer a similar fate and on this day in question my faithful, cake-encrusted Silva compass provided a reliable service. We alighted from the train at Lydford station in the May mid-morning sunshine, although a keen, bordering on the enthusiastic, wind swept across the West Devon plain and persuaded us not to tarry too long savouring the great beauty of the immediate area.

We soon warmed up and proceeded to strip off garments towards the top of Black Down. It was this particular walk which introduced us to the delights of the Tavy Cleave and, as we proceeded along the

The Tavy Cleave - Dartmoor at its best

Reddaford Leat towards it, I was blissfully unaware of the magical land of boulders that lay around the corner of Nat Tor. The overall moorland scene is pleasing to the eye but everyone becomes spell bound when confronted by the Tavy Cleave and its canyon that awaits them. It was only the slide rule constraints of our route planning schedule that forced us to leave.

We scrambled, with great difficulty, up the northern side of the gorge and, apart from a brief stop to photograph the view, made a bee line towards Doe Tor. There were many members of ESHT who, in later life, progressed to become Masters of Puns. Doe Tor started many of them off, 'rabbitting' away. And no, it hasn't got anything to do with the Department of the Environment either!

The fitter members decided to run up Brat Tor to inspect Widgery Cross, whilst my TUF boots felt in need of liquid refreshment and led me down to the Lyd at High Down.

The boundless energy of Mike, Bone and Clive was tested as they had to catch us up whilst we motored past Nodden Gate and up to the weird looking Great Nodden, surely the most unusually shaped hill mass on the moor. The others had seen our ploy and, in their attempt to take a short cut, found themselves on the wrong side of this hill and obliged to climb its most precipitous side. Today it remains a firm favourite for beginner hang gliders who use it as a nursery slope. However, our walk was in the days when thermals were only associated with underwear and not renowned for giving aerial thrills.

Our track was once a railway route that ran up to the Rattlebrook peatworks, an area where the peat cutters often worked in grim conditions to eke out a meagre existence.

Although the railway route contoured back along in a southerly direction, our way lay beneath the side of Corn Ridge or Branscombe's Loaf. The puns returned, sandwiched in a harvest of wit which rolled from our tongues and endured as far as Sourton Tors, a most pleasant pile of rocks with immense views across North West Devon.

Some of Shelstone Tor's local inhabitants

35

Beneath the tors, there was once an ice works which supplied enormous amounts of ice for the Plymouth Fishing Industry. The geography of the site could not have been more suitable, with the alignment of tracks and roads funnelling towards Plymouth, the slopes northward facing away from the sun, and a series of ice-cold springs ideal for channelling into the man-made hollows, or troughs, across the hillside. The ice, when formed, was cut into blocks and transported by horsedrawn carts. The ice was preserved well into May by a cover of bracken or heather. However it should be recorded that the size of these blocks, on arrival at Plymouth's fish quays, was greatly reduced. With the advent of refrigeration, this small industry only lasted about three years.

Before us was the West Okement River and another of those spectacular Dartmoor valleys. We had no idea then that it would later be flooded to make Meldon Reservoir and that, had we followed the same route decades later, a frogman's suit and flippers would have been more useful than a cagoule and walking boots.

By now our company had tired a little and the pun rate was drastically down as we passed under Meldon Viaduct and headed for the

The West Okement Valley before Meldon

gentle path across Okehampton's golf course. The town of Oke-hampton was filled with long shadows and seemed an unwelcoming sight, so we settled down in the quaint waiting room of Okehampton Station whilst we awaited the train to convey us home. Two hours later . . .

6

A Devonshire Walkabout in Cornwall

The built up surroundings on the edge of Devonport are as ugly a scene as anyone might find in Devon. But, at regular intervals each day a motor launch escapes from this twilight zone of urban untidi-ness and heads across the mouth of the Tamar to reach a veritable paradise, on the other side of the river.

With impeccable timing we ran down the short pier onto this, the Cremyll Ferry. As we crossed I told my colleagues of how, in the distant past, it often took five men, about an hour, to row across this short passage, for the winds and currents can be mighty in these parts. One poor lad looked decidedly green as the small vessel rolled and pitched while we crossed to the Cornish bank in blustery conditions.

That day we had planned a walk over the moors, but the thick mist and driving rain prompted us to seek more benevolent conditions. Thus we headed towards the civilised and sheltered delights of the Mount Edgcumbe estate.

Did you know that the patron saint of ferrymen is St Julian? An old boy on the ferry told us this fascinating snippet of information, and went on to tell us of a chapel on the edge of the Mount Edgcumbe estate dedicated to the saint. He claimed that this edifice was only about two yards long and one and a half yards wide, hardly room to store a pair of oars!

The estate is now a country park which provides the people of Plymouth with a wonderful amenity. Although it was dull and wet we passed the Orangery, now a snack bar, and glimpsed all the lovely statues and monuments that adorn the English, French and Italian Gardens. It seems that this park was so beautiful that Duke Medina Sidonia, commander of the Spanish Armada, declared that, after defeating Britain, Mount Edgcumbe would be "his and his

Mount Edgcumbe - my kingdom for a pig?

alone". Fortunately his Spanish eyes never had the opportunity to feast over such a prize.

We found the walk through the park truly relaxing as the gradients were gentle, the scenery easy on the eye and a succession of paths led generally in the direction of Kingsand and Cawsand, our first destinations.

There was once an obelisk, on the edge of the grounds, which bore no inscription but was believed to have been erected in memory of a pig. It seems that a former Countess had a much loved pet pig, called Cupid, whom she loved more greatly than her family. This made her the laughing stock of the aristocracy. However, when the poor creature eventually died, and went to that great bacon factory in the sky, she had the obelisk erected. Now the obelisk has disappeared and in its place there stands the ruin of a folly. Our walkers climbed its spiral staircase for the sake of it, but the view was only a weak and watery one across Plymouth Sound.

From this point the way to Kingsand was extremely easy. The Great Terrace, or Earl's Drive, provided us with a good surface through the woods above the cliff line. Nearer to Kingsand and Cawsand, we came out of the oppressive shade of the woods to glimpse the arc of coastline around to these lovely old villages. The penalty for being out in the open was a comprehensive drenching by

A watery view of Plymouth Sound

a sudden rainstorm, but this only prompted us to move more fleet-footed towards these quaint old settlements.

The grockle (as we call them in Devon) or the emmet (as they call them in Cornwall) is welcome to stick to Looe, Polperro, Mousehole, etc. For in Kingsand and Cawsand there lies the beauty of communities less tarnished by the desire to exploit the legions of trippers

Kingsand - once in Devon, now in Cornwall!

who pour into Cornwall each summer. These settlements are equally beautiful, but fortunately are sufficiently off the beaten track, to remain unspoilt for at least another decade.

Whilst the others had a coffee break, I did a little exploration and engaged some local shopkeepers in conversation. They bemoaned the fact that many of the map makers left this pair of villages off the map, whilst putting on "the decidedly dull and painfully plain" Millbrook which lies "over the hill".

Maritime links abound here and I was told of the great fleet of pilchard boats that worked out of this tiny inlet. At one time the pilchard cellars, just to the north of Kingsand, were full to overflowing and a by-product of this trade was the lighting of the fishermen's cottages by pilchard oil.

I expect it was slightly darker, and quieter, though, when contraband was being landed. In the early 19th century, in this strategic location close to Plymouth, it is claimed that around 20,000 barrels of spirit were landed each year. Certainly a rum business!

On leaving Kingsand we passed, in Garett Street, a curious piece of carved masonry on the wall of a house, for on one side of a line it said "Devon", and on the other it said "Corn". We later discovered that, until 1844, this was the boundary between the two counties. Kingsand was in Devon whilst Cawsand was in Cornwall!

With passports all in order, we crossed this ancient Saxon/Celtic boundary and savoured the equally wonderful delights of Cawsand. There looked to be so many interesting pubs that it was a great shame to pass them by. However, Penlee Point patiently awaited

and we climbed the gently rising track towards it.

We visited Adelaide's Chapel, so named because one of the Earls of Mount Edgcumbe had it constructed for Princess Adelaide (wife of William IV) who had a great affinity with the location. Its harmonious construction does not offend the eye, and we were glad of its shelter on such a fearfully wet and windy day.

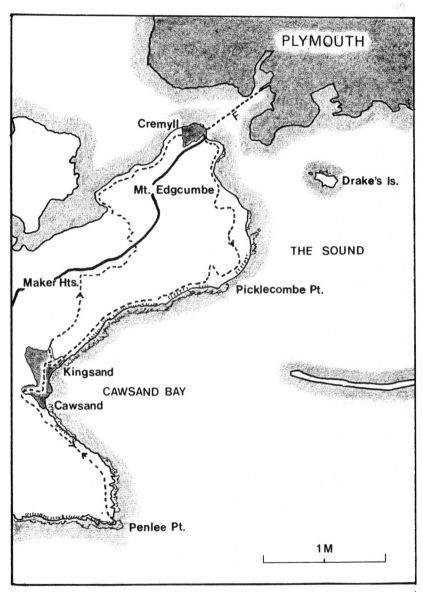

The dotted line from Kingsand back to Cremyll is the way we would have gone if the weather had been more sociable (and the pub less sociable)

41

Indeed the conditions were so inclement—a politer way of describing it than my colleagues suggested—that we decided to abort our intended pilgrimage to the chapel on Rame Head, and returned poste haste to explore the inns and taverns of the twin villages.

Several hours later . . . we emerged not knowing, or caring, whether we had imbibed in ancient Cornwall or pre-Victorian Devon. Mildly stupified we tendered our fares to a patient and tolerant bus driver, who conveyed us back to the Cremyll Ferry. We had missed out on the opportunity to explore the high ramparts of Rame, closest landfall to the Eddystone Reef, but had enjoyed such great hospitality that we vowed to visit this little bit of Devon in Cornwall again one day.

Cawsand - once a notorious haven for smugglers

7
A Walk in the Land of the Dartmoor Devils!

It never ceases to amaze me just how many people flock out from Plymouth, and surrounding districts, into the clear, bracing moorland air at Cadover Bridge. For most it seems to be a blind pilgrimage for they merely congregate for communion at the ice cream carts, or for baptism in the River Plym. Having reached this shrine, they religiously avoid its environs which are left for the "wilderness wanderers" to perambulate in virtual privacy.

Although it was a hot summer's day when we drove past the lunar landscape (china clay spoil heaps) around Lee Moor, it was definitely too early for the masses. Consequently we parked anywhere we liked.

A familiar Dartmoor character adorned another corner of the large car park, namely Godfrey Swinscow, the "king" of the Dartmoor Letterboxers. Godfrey has an infectious enthusiasm for

The River Plym at Cadover Bridge

letterbox safaris, and the great number of fellow boxers around him that June morning was evidence of the popularity of this hobby.

The north bank of the Plym provided the ideal corridor towards the wilder, more remote, parts of the moor. Just beyond Brisworthy Barrows the group were distracted by a topless couple, blissfully unaware of the wide-eyed walkers who, (quite unintentionally!) passed by very closely. At this point I paused to locate a couple of notable landmarks—Legis Tor and Trowlesworthy Tors, of course. I had to insist on moving on, despite unanimous calls for an early lunch break here (it was, after all, only 10 am) and we proceeded, walking backwards, up to Legis Tor.

The going across to Gutter Tor was typical of this corner of the moor, being both gentle in gradient and perfect underfoot for fast walking. Gutter Tor marks an impressive change of scenery. Until this point the views had been away to the South West, across the Lower Tamar, but from here the great basin of Burrator, and its

High on Sheeps Tor's summit

44

towering tors, unveiled itself in all its glory. So many rocky granite cathedrals come into view that the eye is left at a loss which view to enjoy most.

Sheeps Tor rises boldly ahead, but beyond that the impressive Leather Tor peers over its shoulder. Away to the north east a vast number of lesser piles introduce themselves. For the new walker there is a lot to see, and learn, but even those "in the know" are delighted by this ever interesting corner of the moor.

The small valleys which funnel down towards Burrator are all agriculturally enclosed. It is marginal land but sheltered from the worst of moorland weathers. The agrarian usage of the moor influenced our route planning, for there is nothing more irritating than having to scale high stone walls, around fields, decorated by barbed wire fences of Colditz proportions. Throw in a couple of irate farmers, the odd farm bog, some menacing bulls and you have enough evidence to take your party on, what would appear on paper to be, a drunken detour. Likewise that day, we skirted all the fields belonging to Yellowmead and climbed up the back of Sheeps Tor, remaining all the time on open moorland.

Sheeps Tor provides the perfect eyrie from which to sit and contemplate over the most impressive of Dartmoor views. Then we clambered over its enormous rock piles and descended down to Sheepstor Village, only to discover that my rucksack had been left behind on the summit of Sheeps Tor. It was a hot day for extra exercise and the thirst worked up meant a quickening of the pace towards Meavy, and a lunch time pint.

Some respite from the mid day heat was gained in Burrator Wood, which we passed through en route to Yeo Farm. By the side of the road down to Marchant's Bridge, spanning the River Meavy or Mewy, is a cross. This is Marchant's Cross which is no ordinary landmark. In 1291, according to the Charter of Isabella de Fortibus, it is named as Smalacumbacrosse, and was one of the former bondmarks of the lands given, by her mother, to Buckland Abbey a few years earlier. It is reputed that it marked the grave of a suicide victim and, like both Stephen's Grave and Jay's Grave, was located at a crossroads.

Interestingly, medieval wayfarers regularly stopped at this shrine to offer up prayers that they might not face danger on their journey. We scoffed at such superstition, and the thunderbolt from the sky

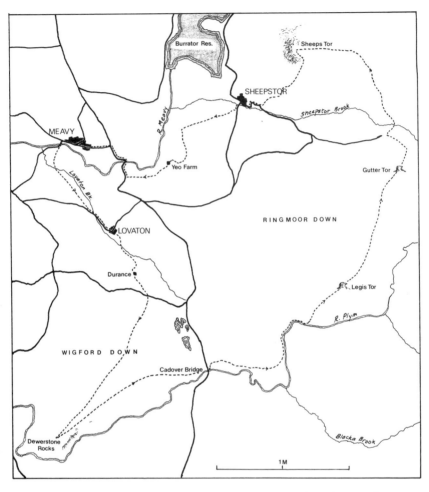

missed us by inches! Joking apart, we soon found ourselves at Meavy, where many bronzed sun worshippers sat on the green outside the Royal Oak. Our late arrival meant that we only had half an hour at the pub, just enough for a quick quart of cool ale.

All too soon we left the Royal Oak and made our way over new territory—turning left towards Lovaton, a hamlet reached by way of a pleasant path.

Admittedly, we may have looked a little worse for wear after our alcoholic indulgences, but we were taken aback by a Lovaton local

Sheepstor Village and Burrator Reservoir

who asked if we knew where we were going! It seems that not many people trek past his cottage so, after convincing him of our intention to be there, we continued up on to Wigford Down on our way towards the Dewarstone.

We avoided some barbed wire fences on the edge of the down, and soon found ourselves on an open common where the going was very easy. The Dewarstone marks the sudden end of Wigford Down. It is a celebrated landmark and attracts climbers from all over the country. The beauty of the rock, from the non-climbers' point of view, is that he or she can attain the summit, without all the nerve jangling antics associated with more vertical elevations. We sat high on a rocky ledge and peered down on the daring deeds of some climbers from the South Devon Club. I reaffirmed my beliefs in self preservation, and maintained that I would never attempt a rock face like that, unless there was a good deal of scaffolding present!

However, a brief factual recall of the origin of the name "Dewarstone" led us to sit a little further from the edge of the cliff. Dewer was another name for the Devil, this time in his capacity as a hunter. His would-be quarries were the souls of unbaptised babies or misbehaving adults (which you can interpret as you like). His pack were called "The Yeth Hounds"—I bet you didn't know the Devil had a lisp! These evil black hounds were employed to drive their

47

On top of Dewarstone, and not a devil in sight!

Cadover Bridge with Shell Top in the distance

victims over the sheer precipice, down into the chasm of the Meavy Valley below.

We turned our backs on the wonderful scene of woods and gigantic rocks and trundled back towards Cadover. The Plym was possibly once called the Cad, hence the appropriate name for Caddaford or Cadover Bridge. On reaching the bridge, we were speechless at the number of cars, and people, which had accumulated there. The scene was dominated by hot people, hot cars, endless queues for ice cream, and a general air of confusion and irritation. At times like this, beauty spots appear to be more like malignant growths!

8

A Bouquet of Barbed Wire at the Mouth of the Erme

In my all-time favourite book, "Under Sail Through South Devon and Dartmoor", Kingston is described, by author Raymond Cattell, as "The end of all creation". If you successfully negotiate the maze of lanes which lead to it, you will begin to see what he meant. Apparently the local pixies, in the guise of the Devon County Council, have taken it into their heads to lead you to Kingston on the "scenic" or indirect route. I use the word scenic advisedly as the hedges are so high that, unless you like hedge views, you are not in for much of a treat!

Eventually arriving, it really was a tremendous relief to get out of our vehicle. Those endless twisting miles of nervous tension, not knowing what was around each sinuous bend, made the thought of a relaxing walk all the more enticing.

Kingston is a delightful mixture of ancient, florally garlanded cottages, varying road widths, interesting corners and differing levels. I believe it has a few inns but only The Dolphin was glimpsed in passing. We parked a short way from the church and left town (a most inappropriate term) along the shallow valley, towards the coast at Westcombe Beach.

The original intention was to do a circular walk and incorporate Bigbury and Burgh Island but, as this was the fourth consecutive day's walking for the group I was leading, there was no way they could be pushed to do a long and arduous ramble. Therefore the gentle path towards Westcombe was the perfect tonic, easy underfoot and all the time dropping towards the coast.

All was well until we reached a small valley dropping down from Scobbiscombe. My old one-inch Ordnance Survey map indicated that the path we were on continued uninterrupted, but reality was different. A small, uncharted lake lay in our path and, in the process of skirting it, we came face to face with one of those so-called 'joys' of walking. The lake's feeder stream, a diminutive watercourse, babbled in a deepish ditch, bordered by a two-tier barbed wire fence. Beyond this, a barrier of nettles, intermingled with thorn and scrub, rose in impenetrable fashion, guaranteed, at best, to annoy and, at worst, to disfigure any intruder.

Some of the party, being of a less hardy disposition, called a pow-wow, and the general consensus of opinion was that a march along the perimeter of the obstacle was preferable. About one hundred yards nearer to Scobbiscombe than we had intended going, a narrow gap appeared. It still bore all the same malevolent facets, but in a scaled down proportion, so we gamely forced our way through. Minutes later, and in the wide fields towards Westcombe Beach, all was forgotten.

This little beach proved to be an exhilarating location as waves of massive power and energy smashed against the cliffs. Glancing at the closeness of the contours, I anticipated a terrific struggle up to Hoist Point. And then I hadn't reckoned with two other factors. The path is dangerously narrow, heavily overgrown and perilously close to the cliff edge and, on the landward side, there is a threatening barbed wire fence. Strangely, while this path has pits, holes and all

Distant Bigbury and Burgh Island

51

manner of difficulties, just beyond the fence the going is firm and would provide the rambler with an easy passage.

At the top of Hoist Point there are tremendous views of the coastline towards Burgh Island and Bigbury. Anyone following in our footsteps will do well to allow for regular breaks at the best vantage points, and for a slow rate of progress, as the path rises and falls with alarming regularity.

Thus at Beacon Point, with many on the verge of submission (and the verge of the cliffs), the scene yields a break in the coastline and the, so far invisible, Erme mouth suddenly appears. It is just above Wonwell that the beauty of the Erme revealed itself to us. The moorland Erme is one of Dartmoor's most beautiful rivers, and this maritime Erme is also a gem in the landscape.

Opposite lies Mothecombe, known for the location filming of "International Velvet". It was wild and desolate, presumably because this was a Thursday and the privately owned beach is only open to the public on Wednesdays, Saturdays and Sundays.

It is worth a cautionary word of warning to wayfarers who might consider a crossing of the Erme at this point. It should only be attempted one hour either side of low tide, at the point where the road down to Wonwell reaches the estuary. Other unfavourable environmental conditions may combine to make this a precarious crossing. Many have been known to take risks here, driven on by the thought that the alternative is a six to ten mile detour, depending whether you cross the footbridge at Holbeton or Sequer's Bridge just west of Modbury on the A379.

Looking at the map, we had not walked very far at all but the look of despair on our pilgrims' faces was enough to cause us to seek a short cut back to Kingston. What fools! From Wonwell Beach there appears, on the map, a path which heads north east directly to the village. This track is ideal, apart from the fact that in places it is stugged in mud, and in others it is thoroughly overgrown. Almost inevitably, it eventually reaches a farm, obviously private property. The farm in this case was Wonwell Court Farm and the anticipated close encounter with an irate farmer turned out to be a much more amiable affair than I could have dared expect. I think he was so surprised that anyone had tried to walk the track, leave alone succeeded in getting through, that he magnanimously allowed us to pass through his farm.

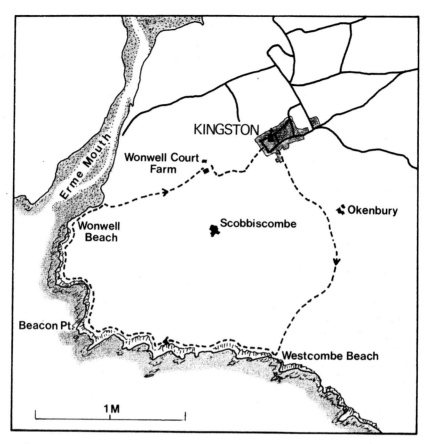

It was late lunch time when we plodded back into Kingston. Somehow an attempt to locate one of Kingston's inns went sadly awry and a kingsized thirst reigned supreme as we left, which, ignoring all the signposts, was the most direct way out of the "end of all creation".

9

Shipley—A Bridge Over Troubled Waters

Definitely something to be wary of in Devon is The Wet Monsoon Season! It can penetrate waterproofs and sink the most buoyant of personalities. It was on just such a dark, dank day in late autumn that we made the voyage through the streamingly wet lanes to Shipley Bridge. There was a secret inner hope that the deluge might stop long enough to enable us to ramble a few miles. But there was soon a grim realisation that wet suits may have been more appropriate gear to wear as a last defence against the driving rain and fierce blustery wind.

It had been a long journey out from Exeter, long in the sense that our 'luxury' conveyance had struggled in fits and starts to reach Shipley Bridge. Jokes about a kangaroo, rather than a tiger, in the petrol tank fell on deaf ears as the driver concentrated on negotiating stray sheep, cattle, Devonshire paced tractors and any other obstacles which lay in our path.

By the time our motley crew reached Shipley Bridge there was a mad rush for the public conveniences, but alas, their relief was short lived when they read the sign on the door, "Closed for the Winter"!

Shipley Bridge had been chosen as it was hoped that the walk up the Avon would be relatively sheltered, and the spectacle of the

torrent thundering down the steeply profiled valley should be an eye catcher. The former theory proved to be totally incorrect, but the latter lived up to expectations. Indeed the valley funnelled the wind straight into our faces.

Within minutes we had passed through the familiar gateposts on the road up to the dam. This was originally a fine house called Brentmoor. Its story is a little sad and is well worth recording.

Brentmoor House was built early in the 19th century for a very wealthy landowner called Meynell. It was the sort of house, in the type of location, that most Dartmoor enthusiasts would dream about. It was

The sign says "Sorry closed for winter due to risk of frost damage"—Spring can seem like a long way away at times!

54

built to last using a good local granite, it also had a fine slate roof and mullioned windows. It had a collection of outbuildings, cowsheds, a dairy, stables, a small cottage, dog kennels and servants' quarters. Indeed this complex was only overshadowed by the empire building designs of Mr Meynell, who upset a lot of the local population with his plan to enclose the lion's share of adjacent Brent Moor. Even so, despite his failure to achieve this, there lies, twixt Knattabarrow and Whitebarrow, a raised bank called "Meynell's Bank".

Mr Meynell's daughter Margaret died at Brent Moor on March 27 1865. Near the main gate is an inscription written beneath the letters MM.

> My lovely little Lilly
> Thou wert gathered very soon
> In the fresh and dewy morning
> Not in the glare of noon.
> The Saviour sent his angels
> To bear thee hence, my own
> And they'll plant thee in that garden
> Where decay is never know.

There is another story which says that the poor girl was buried here as it was impossible to get to church because of bad weather. Today the setting for the memorial may seem strange as it lies overshadowed by a jungle of rhododendrons. But where it was set up, it was close to an attractive lily pond in a well landscaped garden.

The next owner, Rear Admiral John Tuke, kept the well staffed house in excellent order. Bathing must have been an invigorating experience as the water was pumped directly from the river to the bathroom. Fortunately John Tuke was a good Victorian Christian who would have enjoyed a bracing bath—the waters of the Avon, in winter, are somewhat chilly. I can just imagine his yell, "Geronimo" before plunging into his refreshing(!) bath.

William Ambrose Pritchard, a rich and fat man, who frequently boasted that he had never done a day's work in his life, became the next owner. He had a prediliction for breeding Irish terriers and is known to have been so upset by damage to his garden, caused by white cabbage butterflies, that he paid children for jarfulls of a hundred or more of these pests.

John Pritchard eventually also managed to drive out several members of the family, including his wife and children and ended his days alone and unloved. The family treasures were auctioned and the house became a Youth Hostel for a while. When the Avon Dam was being built the waterboard used the house as offices but, in its semi derelict state, it became a target for vandals and succumbed to the relentless wiles of Dartmoor weather. The house had all but died when a devastating military exercise contrived to reduce the house to ruins.

Rather than relate this sad story to my increasingly wet compatriots, I settled for showing them an unusual tree growing out of one of the former walls of the house.

The well made path which winds up the valley to the dam is a popular avenue on fine days. It is common to see pushchairs and convoys of prams trundling along. However that day it was so wet and wild that the only people in the Dartmoor wilderness were the spartan brigade, fiendish fans and dedicated devotees of "The Great Outdoors".

At the dam, great torrents cascaded over the dam wall causing massive waves in the plunge pool below. We climbed to the top of

The Avon Dam - on good days you can walk a pram there, but on wet days a submarine is more appropriate!

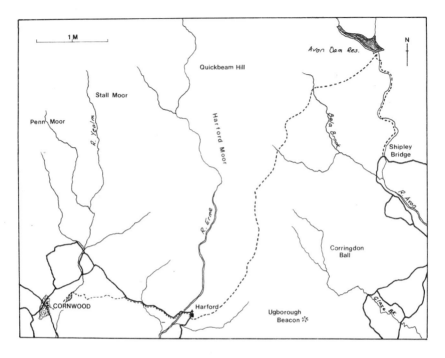

the dam and, as we peered over the top, it appeared as if the elements had gone completely mad with enormous waves crashing against the barrier of the dam.

Standing up was a difficult task and we cursed the fact that we had instructed the coach to go on to Cornwood. All intentions to go to Red Lake and Ducks' Pool were immediately cancelled out and, snuggled in the lee of the dam, we made contingency plans.

Everybody was making good use of their wet weather equipment, to such an extent that it was difficult to recognise anyone. All that could be seen were eyes peering out from protecting hoods, bala-clavas and the like. Several had taken glucose to give them energy whereas others reduced their resistance to the elements by consuming the contents of their hip flasks. Thus, with Dutch courage, it was agreed that a fast pace be maintained, and no stops entertained, until Harford Church was reached.

And so it was—heads down, a good rhythm of pace about three and a half miles per hour, and the wind blowing across our paths, we weaved our way across Zeal Hill, under Hickley Plain, past

Harford Church on a more benign day

Hobajohn's Cross and down to Harford via Harford Moor Gate. The worst ten minutes were near Glaze Head when its name bore more significance than I care to remember. A furious downpour of extremely large hail stones hit us so hard that an abundance of rich vocabulary, that is completely unprintable, resounded across the moor. Despite protective headwear, the hail stones really hurt and carpeted the moor in a layer of ice.

The sanctuary of the church at Harford was greatly appreciated, as was the appearance of our flasks of coffee and a revival of conversation. It had been impossible to talk in the wind so we all had a lot of catching up to do. Needless to say, safe and dry, the perils of our predicament were magnified and we were all heroes in our own eyes on the road walk to Cornwood, so we toasted ourselves with a jar or three at its inn. And if I'm not mistaken, I do believe we drank Courage!

Cornwood where we drowned our sorrows after our sorrows had nearly drowned us

---
10
Around The Haldon Hills

Sometimes the more usual walking areas seem unappealing, like when a strong blustery wind is blowing across the wide open spaces of the moor. On such occasions a stroll on lanes and paths is far more therapeutic, especially after a sequence of walks involving thorough soakings, across miles of mire or 'sublime slime'.

On this occasion, we had contrived to choose the Sunday when the clocks had been advanced one hour to British Summer Time, giving us an extra hour of daylight at the end of the day, a useful asset if you are lost at dusk. That is, provided that the entire team remember to adjust their watches!

One of the crew suggested a starting point that he knew well from his courting days (but not for walking)—that is the wooded hill of Haydon Common (SX 931833) near Kenn. The small twisting lane which ran from Kenn appeared to be a strangely unfamiliar route for our friend, even though he had driven along it on many occasions. Obviously things look different in daylight!

We took the ridge track from Haydon Common which leads south-westwards up on to the Haldon Hills. Beneath us to our left was the lovely secluded valley of Oxton but, as our climb was long and quite steep, we did not linger long to savour the view, although we did notice large fields to our left and small ones to our right.

A vast amount of the top of the Haldon escarpment is covered in woodland, which doesn't appeal to many mountaineers. However on

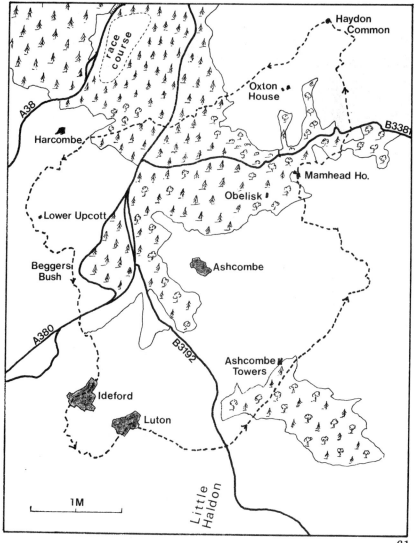

windy days, such as this, the shelter is always welcome and the pure aromatic air a joy to inhale.

The navigation over the next mile or so could only be described as masterful. We weaved along tracks through the woods with a dogged determination not to be lured off our route by the endless variety of thoroughfares open to us. We descended into Harcombe (meaning Hare Valley) on a good track which ultimately led us to Harcombe House, once owned by a family called Balle, who were related to the Balles of Mamhead in the seventeenth century. Harcombe House is now a rest home for "burnt out" firemen.

Just before reaching the trout and carp lakes of Harcombe, we veered off a path towards Waddon (the hill of woad). Waddon, centuries ago, was a more important settlement than it is today. Its former importance was attributable to its location on an old trade route. Legend has it that a couple of dishonest folk, who ran the inn, were suspected of theft when merchants reputedly lost items of their property whilst staying there. After sufficient proof against them was had, the couple were charged with theft and publicly executed in Exeter.

This cheerful little saga accompanied us past Waddon and Beggars Bush. At this point we were confronted by the dangerous prospect of following the A380. This stretch is Devon's answer to Brand's Hatch, with one-way traffic hurtling along around the enormous chicane leading to Thorn's Cross.

To avoid this potential death trap, we descended into the valley where Dunscombes Farms are located, and emerged on the A380 at a point beyond the hazard and we safely crossed the road. A few fields and hedges later, we reached the lane on the edge of Ideford Common where John James' gypsy encampment is located. Before us, to the south, lay the best views of the day, towards the Teign estuary and Milber Downs, high above Newton Abbot. The last few hundred yards had been a struggle, but the way ahead down into lovely Ideford was more than an adequate compensation.

The welcome at the Royal Oak is always friendly and our merry band soon felt at home. We had a marvellous time looking around at the many strange and fascinating items housed in the bar.

I had often heard of the beauty of Well Covert (also referred to as Ideford Combe), a valley just to the south west of Ideford. At the expense of missing a prolonged stay at The Royal Oak, we left in

The Royal Oak at Ideford snuggled beneath Haldon Moors

The diminutive Larcombe Bridge

order to savour the new delights of this hidden valley. We ventured out of the end of a lane leading away from Ideford and paused awhile at the beautifully diminutive Larcombe Bridge—Larcombe means the valley where the wild iris grows (but not today). From this point we could see the densely wooded slopes of Well Covert. However, a sudden realisation that it was "twenty to closing time" triggered a sudden unanimous urge to change our route.

A most pleasant footpath was thus followed to the Elizabethan Inn (SX 903769) in the hamlet of Luton. The valley which houses this small community has been in the hands of the Vooght family ever since William of Orange rewarded one of his physicians, a Vooght, with this land as a gift. The Vooghts now run three farms in and around Luton.

Soon, after downing the swiftest of pints, we were climbing the shoulder of Little Haldon, initially by lane but later by the open heath covered moorland. It is hard to believe that plateau once had an aerodrome where many rallies were held and several dignitaries, including the Prince of Wales, once landed.

The Great Western Railway even had their own passenger service with a small plane painted in the same livery as their railway carriages. They advertised the service as Railway Air Services. From Little Haldon they operated various routes at differing times to Cardiff, Birmingham, Plymouth, Portsmouth and other English

Haldon Aerodrome's old Remains. Once a Land of Flying Trains!
(Top that Rupert the Bear?)

Looking from Little Haldon towards Dartmoor

locations. The age of the plane was primarily the 1930s on Little Haldon and little aerial activity took place after the second World War. It was regarded as the dustiest take off runway in Britain! All that now remains are a few derelict buildings, all fast decaying.

From lofty Little Haldon the views are magnificent. The long arm of Southern Dartmoor reaches out towards the South Hams, whilst the hordes at Haytor peer down at us. To the east the coastline tails away, first with deep red cliffs, and then in the bold white of chalk which fades away to the thinnest of lines towards Portland Bill. But there is more to the view than that, and each chosen vista excites the eye.

Knowing that some of Teignmouth's golfers are not exactly Tom Watson standard, more slices than a family sized cut loaf, we avoided traversing the golf course.

We left this little moor via Castle Dyke and the road past Ashcombe Tower. After a half mile along this gentle wooded drive we forked off downhill to Broom House. Now we had entered the semi sub tropically warm valley of Dawlish Water, hidden in this section from all those wicked winds that wreak so much havoc on high ground. We headed straight across the cross roads and climbed up to Mamhead, the teat-shaped hill. But this was no dummy run. This was proven by the unanimous vote to avoid the precipitous haul up to the Obelisk known as Mamhead Point. If you would like to know more about this monument, I suggest you buy "Around and About the Haldon Hills".

Our rearranged route took us through Mamhead Park where we passed the miniature church, muttering, "Forgive us our trespasses", and we took the eastward path down to Mamhead. From there, we briskly lane walked in almost a straight line, apart from the twists and turns, across the B3381 and anon towards Oak and Ash Farms.

By now we had almost gone full cycle and our pedals, or feet, after this 12 mile romp, were glad to reach our vehicle on Haydon Common just as nightfall was about to set in. Had it not been British Summer Time, we would have had the last few miles in the dark!

11

A Princetown Perambulation

Burrator is Dartmoor's oldest, biggest and most beautiful reservoir. Beside it, great stands of coniferous trees clothe the steep hillsides in many shades of green. Above this, great peaks rise skywards to silhouette the horizon with impressive rocky grandeur. It is a serene environment from whence to commence a walk, the only problem is that you invariably have a steep and demanding climb to reach open moorland, unless of course you opt for one of the tracks down into the Meavy Valley.

We had every intention of scaling Sheepstor, perhaps the mightiest challenge from the water's edge, but the early morning blues, following a late night of revelry, demanded a more pastoral and gentle start to the day.

Our party, numbering four—the optimum minimum group size suggested by those who know all about how to walk in complete safety, was made up of two teachers, a policeman and a computer programmer.

We left the track from Burrator and went and sat down on the steep shores of Crazy Well Pool, or, as the teachers in our party preferred, "Classiwell Pool", an early variation in its place name. The pool is believed to possess secret powers of dark persuasion, and is also believed to be bottomless. It sounds an excellent spot to take errant pupils! Late in the last century some pyromaniac or arsonist set fire to the steep banks leading down to this pool. The ground was so badly scorched, by the heathland holocaust, that it was several decades before the vegetation regenerated to its normal cover.

After a refreshing coffee stop, we resumed our walk. We followed the Devonport Leat, a gentle gradient with easy conditions underfoot, to take us on towards Nun's Cross Farm. Here, a century ago, John Hooper took on the excesses of moorland weather, and a difficult terrain, to turn this farm into a temporarily successful venture. The word 'successful' in this context merely means 'survived' for many years, despite all the odds. His meagre living, hard won from a grudging moor, was not enough to woo others to such a harsh environment. I was amused by the present state of accommodation on offer. Obviously there must be warmer nights than I thought in these parts as, when we inspected the garden, there were several old bedsteads standing beneath the hedge.

We dismissed the thought of a quick nap and continued on our leat long excursion to The Whiteworks. Clive recalled an Army organised manhunt, in which he took part, several years ago. Having gained the sanctuary of The Whiteworks at nightfall, his group bedded down here. Later, in the dead of night, one of his crew, a known somnambulist, arose, sinisterly took a dagger from a drawer and plunged it into a floorboard, inches away from Clive's head! Bizarrely, the following morning they discovered some unused death certificates in an old chest. Incidentally,the would-be assassin is now a policeman, walking the beat.

We did not wish to linger at Whiteworks and Clive, in particular, was keen to get on the way past Peat Cot and along the Castle Road towards Princetown. On this track we paused at Tor Royal, a pioneering attempt to convert a large pocket of moorland into a thriving agricultural area. The patron, of this miniature Dartmoor

The Whiteworks with Foxtor Mires beyond

agrarian revolution, was Thomas Tyrwhitt (1762-1833), close friend
of the Prince of Wales, (George, Prince Regent). It was partly this
bond which led to the community being named Princetown. For a
while, Tyrwhitt's dream looked like being realised but, after a few
years, the moorland weather again depleted crops, and the project
was all but abandoned.

Just over the hill, down on the West Dart at Prince Hall, another

An old aerial view of Princetown

pioneering experiment was undertaken long ago. A farmer here introduced Scottish sheep to Dartmoor for the first time. His name just happened to be Lamb—would I try to pull the wool over your eyes?

We reached Princetown at the perfect moment—opening time. Although it was only a matter of minutes after midday, The Plume of Feathers was already packed. The reason for the multitudes being there was the weekly folk club, held every Sunday lunch time, when various musicians are called on to entertain in what must be the liveliest spot on Dartmoor.

We left in high spirits to return to Burrator. As enthusiasts of

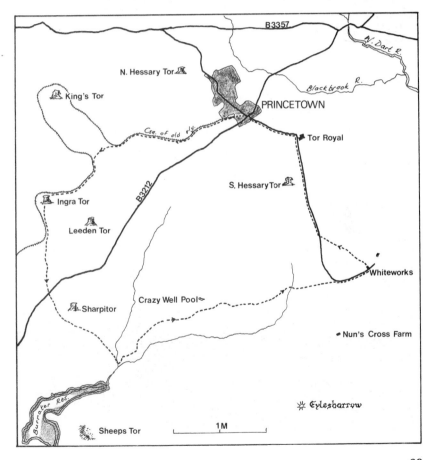

Another old view - Yelverton Station and the train has long since departed from here!

industrial archaeology, we decided to follow the track bed of the former Yelverton to Princetown branch line. Because it was tedious strolling along on the hard clinker, we opted to walk on the springy turf beside the line. This line once provided a vital link with the outside world, but closed on 5 March 1956.

Burrator Reservoir - water, water all around and not a tree in sight!

70

On the map the route appears to follow a crazy weaving pattern, so sinuous in its curvaceousness that the trains were sentenced to completely encircle some of the hills before getting up to Princetown. We carefully cut off the most tortuous of these contouring detours to drop down to Ingra Tor Halt, now just a memory. The trains, platforms, and passengers are no more. However, its place in the annals of railway history is assured, as it once bore a sign warning passengers to "Beware of Adders". Perhaps "Beware of Transport Minister" (who axed this line) may have been a more apt message.

We stayed with the line as far as we dared and soon dropped into the woods around Burrator Reservoir. The two teachers chalked up another successful walk, Policeman Mike, a law unto himself, needed 'A rest', and poor old Pete Tyers, the computer operator, very much the 'basic' Dartmoor walker, was 'worn' out and deflated!

12

A South Hams Safari—To Dartmoor By The Sea

Where is Chivelstone you may ask? If you blinked on driving through, you would certainly miss it. To find it you should head southwards from either Frogmore or Chillington (A379) and you ought to reach Chivelstone after two and a half miles. As you might guess, not many people pass through this rural backwater of the South Hams. However, we went to great pains, with endless reversing in the minibus over alpine type hills, to get there, to this hamlet of few houses and an attractive church, in order to find a wide verge on which to park our vehicle.

Despite the fact that Chivelstone is a few miles from the coast, its church has, at times, been involved in maritime events. In December 1868 eight bodies from the wreck of the *Gossamer* were laid to rest in the belfry. For whom the bell tolls?

Surprisingly, on a day when most of Devon enjoyed a real scorcher, we were doomed to labour beneath grey skies in a heavy, thundery atmosphere. But the company was good, spirits were high, and the flesh willing, well almost!

From Chivelstone Cross we headed south on the road towards Prawle but, fearing for our lives in the hands of daredevil tractor

71

drivers, we headed on to a south east aligned farm track. This is a typically South Hams affair, apparently long forgotten by backpackers, for it is overgrown by a riot of vegetation. Within its high banks live a little universe of insects, moths and butterflies. To add to the misery of the oppressive atmosphere, the over-numerous population of flies took a distinct liking to our sweaty carcasses. This meant that we walked faster to extricate ourselves from the hedgerow torture. The vicious circle continued with an increase in perspiration from extra exertion, and made complete by more flies attracted, to get away from which, we had to walk faster! Walking can be so much fun!

At the first crossroads of tracks (Higher Borough) we turned right and walked to Woodcombe, with its striking chimney breast, obviously well stacked. A well intentioned farmer suggested that the best way to East Prawle was to cross the Barley field, following the line of telegraph poles. He was right although, in a dip along the way, the vegetation cover was somewhat impenetrable. Low budget film makers could easily adapt it for jungle films. Tarzan visits East Prawle?

The latter is an unusual village, perched on a small plateau high above the sea. It has a fine inn called the Pig's Nose, which probably takes its name from the coastal feature of the same name about a mile west of the village. Observant folk will also detect Gammon Head, Ham Stone, Bullock Cove, and The Bull. Perhaps this is why the area is called the South Hams?

East Prawle has a somewhat drab, grey appearance through its use of local building stones. It is however brightened up by its telephone box, complete with Salcombe Ferry times, and its bus shelter with a weather vane on top.

From this curious settlement, we fell away to the coastline at Prawle Point, Devon's most southerly headland, its name deriving from an old Saxon word meaning 'look out point'. To the east, the coastline looked most appealing with its two tier line of cliffs. Alas, no ale house lay towards Start Point and, as the Gara Rock Hotel had been duly noted as an alcoholic oasis, there seemed little point in crossing such splendid rocky pinnacles as Lobeater Rock or The Torrs. Indeed the coastline north westwards from Prawle is indescribably beautiful. Dartmoor by the Sea would be the best compliment. This orgy of rock and wave had me delving into my

Dartmoor by the Sea

rucksack for my camera, in a frantic bid to convert this scenery into photographic proof of its awesome loveliness.

Everybody enjoyed the next few miles above Black Cove and Macely Cove, en route to the reptilian shaped bastion of Gammon Head. I must have taken at least twenty snaps in this mile long romp. Despite the hair raising nature of the walk, the path itself was firm and safe and permitted a good rate of progress.

Beyond Gammon Head, the coastline continues with unnerving undulation. Almost mesmerised by the Gammon Head/Prawle Point section, I hardly noticed the Pig's Nose or Deckler's Island as our party thirstily hastened towards the Gara Rock Hotel, high on the cliffs above Abraham's Hole.

As we approached the Hotel from below, it appeared like a fort, resembling the type that the cavalry used in defending themselves against renegade red indians. It even had a flag pole with a Union Jack. However, there was no John Wayne to greet us and, on closer inspection, the main part of the complex bore no real resemblance to any last outpost.

We had done it! The most southerly hotel in Britain's loveliest county had been visited, and only a brief glimpse was needed to see that this was a lovely place in which to stay. Originally the small

73

cliff-top community here grew up to keep watch on the coastline for wrecks and for smugglers. Indeed, this coastline has long been a graveyard for ships. Amongst many ships wrecked on Gara Rock was a French vessel called *Touquet* which came to grief in April 1934. But its "grief" ended three days later when it was refloated.

Some of our hale and hearty walkers had earlier satisfied their hunger pangs by eating their packed lunches at the mouth watering Gammon Head. Thus they consulted the menu at the Gara Rock Hotel, with ravenous intentions of indulging in a further feast. I could not help but smile at some of the items on offer for, appropriately, there appeared Trawlerman's Pot, Coastguard's Lunch, and, would you believe, "Gara"-baldi submarine sandwich! Even the soup was modestly called "Jolly Good Soup", and I expect it was.

At the Hotel there is an album, available for public inspection, which tells the story of the hotel from its pre-hotel days to the present day. At one time the land belonged to Blundell's School, Tiverton. In the garden is a former "look out" point for the coastguard. More recently it was converted to be the smallest licensed premises in Britain, only to be thwarted by the antics of petty bureaucrats who found a way to prevent further trading.

Amongst the residents, who were in the bar, was a group of very well groomed young men and well manicured young ladies. We later discovered that they were there for 3 days to shoot photographs for the fashion section of a well known Mail Order Catalogue. I won't say which one, but there weren't many little woods on these cliffs to make them feel at home.

Thus, with our thirst for beer and local knowledge well quenched, we set off around Rickam Common, a former golf course, to enter the Kingsbridge estuary near Salcombe.

Sunny Cove failed to live up to its name, although there were a number of optimistic sun seekers who sat in anticipation of any solar activity, but I doubt whether they ever took their coats off.

We strolled on at a good pace on the metalled road past the Salcombe/East Portlemouth Ferry and on towards South Pool creek. The Kingsbridge Estuary is the perfect example of what geographers refer to as a ria or drowned river valley. Such a feature is the result of a change in sea levels. Former levels, higher and lower, are marked by raised beaches and submerged forests. South Devon has more than its share of each. The Kingsbridge Estuary has the

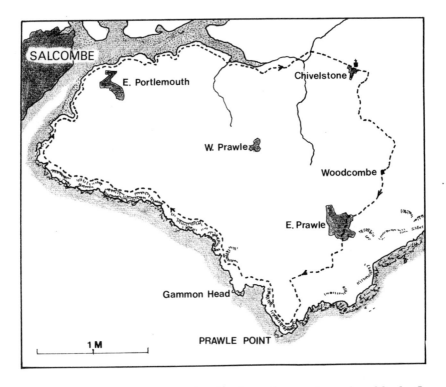

classic fingered appearance of a ria where the creeks end suddenly. I was so wrapped up in this discourse of geographical phenomena, that I forgot to photograph it.

The road walking section, around the base of these high and steep sided hills, was a somewhat tedious affair. By the time we had reached the hamlet of Goodshelter, many of our backpackers had become fatigued. Eleven hard miles had been completed and they unanimously felt that the best way they could refresh their sagging spirits, was to paddle in the ice cool waters of Waterhead Creek.

Rehabilitated, the ensemble struggled onwards towards Chivelstone. Many thought that it was unfair that we could not avail ourselves of a short cut, on a public right of way, from Waterhead as it was clearly shown on all our maps. A young lad at Waterhead claimed it had been unused for years, and thus a prolonged roadwalk completed our stroll. What a shame that the Seven Stars Inn at Chivelstone no longer existed, for we could have drunk it dry!

75

13

From Ashburton To Chagford And Back
On Shanks's Pony

Nostalgia has got a lot to answer for! For many people it means rides on steam trains, visits to historic sites, battlefields, trips down caves and so on. From a walker's viewpoint, nostalgia means following old routes, like the Abbots' Way and The Tom Cobley walk, etc.

When researching Chagford's past, I came across many references to the vast amount of traffic, of files of packhorses, which carried lime to Chagford or wools back to Ashburton. The question which proved difficult to answer was, "Which way did they go?" This original thought then germinated into an excuse for another marathon walk, designed to satisfy my curiosity about the nature of the terrain between the two settlements.

The friends who accompanied me did so because of their desire to get fit, and they also shared my enthusiasm to see parts of the National Park which we did not visit too often. In a long walk you can build a more comprehensive appreciation of the topography. And the resultant exploration went something like this.

Ashburton was sleeping as we parked in the large, free car park where the old pannier market once stood. It was a brilliant, sunny June morning. As the town is in a natural bowl of the hills, the only way out is up. Within minutes of commencing the roadwalk, a never-ending upwards struggle to Ausewell Cross, the others had persuaded me not to stick with the probable road walk, but to follow open moorland wherever possible. We therefore followed a reasonably direct route to Chagford, so that, on the return much later, we could deviate knowing there was sufficient energy, and stamina, left to cope with it.

From Ausewell Cross we scurried across a few fields and sat down on Buckland Beacon to recover. After all, in two and a half miles, we had scaled over a thousand feet, an average gradient of 1:13 (about 8%) for almost an hour. Climbs like this, in June, are best done in the early morning or late evening, when the air is cooler.

The next part of the walk was probably the most enjoyable as we crossed Blackslade, or Ruddycleave Water, and headed over Wittabarrow, to reach Pil and Top Tors without too much effort. Gentle

Ashburton

slopes and firm, easy ground made this a pleasant stretch. Having experienced, before, the mega-misery of wallowing in nearby Black-slade Mire, it was reassuring to be above that sodden cesspit of a bog. Spend half an hour there, and you will appreciate why words are not minced on any descriptive analysis of its finer qualities.

Bonehill Rocks is such a pleasing-to-the-eye pile of rocks that it has attracted film makers—The Hound of the Baskervilles and

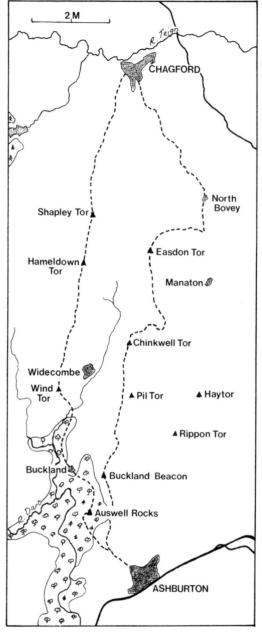

Jamaica Inn are just two filmed on location there. Those readers of such fiction will be aware that Jamaica Inn is actually on Bodmin Moor, and this shows how film makers are not above bending the facts a little.

We scaled our favourite mini mountain range of tors, Bell, Chinkwell and Honeybag Tors before traversing some fields to reach Jay's Grave. Beyond this was a short burst of northwards road walking past Heatree Cross and soon we had scaled the isolated triangular shaped hill which bears the name of Easdon Tor.

At North Bovey it was observed that the Ring o' Bells had just opened for custom and, as there were no customers, we took pity on the landlord and had half a pint, just to be sociable. We restricted this to about two minutes, for we were keen to get on to Chagford.

The extent of farms forced us to walk the country lanes, but this

The village green at North Bovey

The Square, Chagford

was no chore as they were quiet and gave good views of the immediate landscape. We reached Nattadon Common, a lovely little moor above Chagford, and were duly impressed with the view towards Castle Drogo and the Teign Gorge.

By now it was 12.30 pm, we had covered about 14 miles and deserved our meal at The Three Crowns in Chagford. In the entrance to the hotel, during the Civil War, a greatly respected local man, Sidney Godolphin, was shot in the upper leg, and died immediately. Another victim of a shooting, in the same era, was Mary Whiddon who was shot dead at her wedding. A jealous friend committed the dastardly deed, on which Blackmore supposedly based his world famous novel, Lorna Doone. The two bars at the Three Crowns Hotel are named after these two unfortunate people.

I like to remember Chagford for its contribution to Dartmoor Walking. As the railway network crept towards Chagford, the town developed a fine reputation for hunting, fishing, shooting and walking holidays. But the railway companies never got as far as Chagford itself, although elaborate plans were made to bring a line up to Chagford Bridge via the Teign Gorge. It was commonplace for the elite of the London social circles to pay a day trip to Chagford. The nearest railway station was Moretonhampstead, Chagford's deadly

rival, and the last stage of the journey was completed in a pony and trap. Later, in its stead, came Devon's first public bus service, run by the LSWR, from Exeter.

Out of its popularity as a resort, great guides like James Perrot emerged. He owned a fishing tackle business and reputedly knew every inch of Dartmoor. He is remembered for his inauguration of Dartmoor's first "Letterbox" at Cranmere Pool in 1854. He deposited a bottle there, and people on walks to this wilderness left their calling cards. I wonder what he would think today with "letterboxes" virtually everywhere, over 500 of them, with the original calling card now replaced by a rubber stamp. The drawing depicts James Perrot waiting to be picked up, by horse and trap, before going up to Fernworthy to lead a guided walk. Behind him you will see a building called The Shambles, now replaced by Chagford's most noted landmark in the Square.

Still on the theme of transport, I noticed the familiar face of veteran char-a-banc driver, Dougie Gourd from Bishopsteignton, who, despite his great age, was still carrying passengers in his own inimitable style. I asked him if I could take his photograph, and he obliged with some unusual poses! After this picture was taken, he got out his watering can and played a few songs on it—very entertaining!

We had a good meal at The Three Crowns but could just as easily

The legendary coach driver, Mr Dougie Gourd of Bishopsteignton, who likes to keep a beady eye (or two) on his passengers!

have gone to The Ring o' Bells or The Bullers Arms (originally the Bakers Arms) as they all provide excellent value.

The hustle and bustle of Chagford life was soon left behind as we skirted the enormous Meldon Hill. Earlier this century it had a golf course around it, and traces can still be seen. Mr Webber has an original sign, proving its existence, at his shop in the Square.

It is most unlikely that any teams of packhorses would have crossed this precipitous hill. We did because it lay in a direct line with Jurston, a point that we wished to reach so that we could pick up the Mariners Way. We only followed part of this route (which linked North Devon to the South coast) between Jurston and Moor Gate. At the latter we made a direct line for the great humpbacked hill of Hameldown.

Once we reached the elevated Hameldown Tor, the next miles

Just one of many fine rock piles found on Meldon Hill high above Chagford

were easy. We made excellent progress past its beacon and down to Wind Tor. The East Webburn was crossed at Cockingford. Our route took us through the small caravan site here, where we were engaged in conversation with an enthusiastic moor walker, down on his annual pilgrimage from the Midlands.

We continued our stroll through the woods to Buckland in the Moor. After a short section of road walking, we returned to the woodland paths near Ausewell Rocks and swooped down into Ashburton with great gusto.

This walk certainly wasn't the struggle probably experienced by the files of packhorses. But then again, the packs we carried were four-packs of light ale. Our pedometer revealed that we had covered 30 miles, at an average of 10 miles per pint!

— 14 —
A Dart Around Start Point

After negotiating miles of tortuously twisting lanes, we arrived at the coastal settlement of Beesands. To get to this magical place is a Mystery Tour, but it is certainly no joy trip! The small community knows both the joy and despair of being such close neighbours with the sea, which would lap against its front doors, if not protected by a substantial barrier of enormous boulders. In a westerly gale, Beesands is snugly tucked away in the lee of high hills and has no cause for concern. But when an easterly blast blows, long and hard over the extensive open stretch of water to the east, the little community must lend more than an interested eye to the proceedings.

But today the sea was like a millpond and, although it was only April, the sky was deep blue and the air warm, as it often is in this subtropical part of Devon. From the long line of houses that constitutes Beesands, the smoke rose from the chimneys in neat vertical lines, evidence of the still conditions. As we walked in good spirits along this promenade, not a soul stirred, for who could not be at peace in such wonderful surroundings?

After a brief hibernation since the last bout of arduous exercise, the initial slope out of Beesands, on the way marked 'Coastal Path', caused some heavy breathing.

Tinsey Head does not rise or protrude unduly, and only the discerning navigator will have cause to remark on its passing. Initially, we found the path easy on the feet but, as it begins to fall at Green-straight, it is overgrown in places and we had to beware of, what threatened to be, defacing and disfiguring vegetation.

Miraculously unscathed, we descended into the small valley which drops from the hills, past the delightful sounding farm called Muckwell. In westerly gales this is a draughty venue. In the days when flares, or bell bottomed trousers, were all the rage, we had some laughs here as great gusts of wind would inflate our trouserwear ito balloon proportions. I recall one spindly little fellow in our company, almost got blown into the sea. With a sail hoisted, I'm sure he could have reached France!

This hollow is not without interest. At one time it bore a ley or lake built up behind the shingle bar. However the steady input of silt, brought down by its feeder stream, caused it to fill up. Other leys along this shore line have either silted up, are silting up or will silt up. This particular one has great long reeds growing from its swamp, which have been used locally for basket making. The withies were also ideal for making crab pots. The latter was particularly important, as the shallow nature of the sea floor across Start Bay is the perfect environment for crabs, and other associated marine beasties.

For centuries the small fishing communities along Start Bay

derived their livelihood by catching crabs, and other related species of crustacean, and sending them to high class restaurants as far away as the Midlands and London. As the crabbing industry declined, the fishermen began to feel the pinch!

As we crossed the stream on the beach at Hallsands, we looked hard and long at the North Hallsands Hotel and tried to think of a reason for stopping. Finally we had to settle on "thirst". It was so usual to excuse our constant delays in the name of 'research' into local history, etc. that we had developed a phobia over admitting the more simple reason for such a stop. But then, once inside, we noticed the walls were decorated with many pictures of celebrated theatre and television personalities. What an education!

The next quarter mile of coast has been severely eroded by the elements. On the cliff top we passed a line of holiday lets which, in a few years, may well be *in* the sea and not beside it! The route of the path has been altered to avoid some dangerous subsidence.

The old village school, a humble, shack-like affair, looked derelict and warned folk to stay away. Beyond this is Trout's holiday apartments, originally a hotel but, following the trend towards self catering accommodation, endured a change of status. The Trouts are well known in this vicinity. Ella Trout performed an act of great bravery, in the First World War, by rowing out and rescuing a drowning mariner from a torpedoed ship, despite the presence of U boats. The parents of the saved man rewarded her with money, with which the Trout's building was constructed.

The ruins at Hallsands in Start Bay

In a short distance we had descended the narrow lane down to the site where Hallsands Village once stood. All that remains are a few stubborn walls that will soon crumble and be washed away, in much the same way that the thirty or so houses were destroyed in the great storms of late January 1917.

Some casual visitors to Hallsands' ruins, or "How to get my entire family into one picture in my book without it looking too obvious"

It was decided in 1894 that dredgers should remove a half million tons of shingle from just off the shore at Hallsands. This vital raw material was needed in the construction of new docks at Keyham, Plymouth. It was predicted, by the dredging authorities, that the natural anti-clockwise currents of Start Bay would soon replace the extracted shingle. It didn't. Hallsands' problems were acute because the natural protection, against highly destructive waves, was its beach and this was dropping in its level. There were gradual signs that all was not as it should be. Wilson's Rock, which originally just peeped above the sands, became greatly exposed. Each time an easterly or north easterly gale blasted at this small community, more devastation resulted. Running repairs and temporary measures enabled the settlement to survive until 1917. I told the group about my childhood recollection of meeting Elizabeth Prettejohn, the last resident of the village to stay on the narrow shelf beneath the cliffs. Her house was slightly raised above the others and remains, almost as a monument, to the passing of a genuine fishing village, and a reminder of the folly of fellow man.

Incredibly the coast holds other gems and, as the company were eager to see Start Point, we followed the gently rising path up to the small car park above the headland. There are two ways to the Light-

The derelict chapel at Hallsands awaits a watery baptism as the cliff recedes

house. There is the comfortable, easy to follow tarmac road, and there is the scramble across the lizard-like rocky pinnacles. Naturally, as adventurers we fully enjoyed the latter.

Start gets its name from an Anglo-Saxon word which means 'tail'. It too has a history. Its lighthouse has stood there since 1836, issuing its warning light to the countless thousands of ships which pass safely by each year. Less fortunate are those ships which have foundered there. In 1891, during a great blizzard, the *Marana* was wrecked with the loss of 22 people. This included some who survived the wreck, but froze to death on the cliffs.

Another person to 'finish at the Start' was the pirate, Henry Muge, who was hanged there and left to rot in chains as a warning to others.

Peartree Point, the next headland, was passed and the temptation to have a romp on the golden beaches at Great Mattiscombe (pronounced Matchcombe) was one to which we almost fell. Be warned—the tidal race around Start approaches Grand Prix proportions, and even fishes nearly drown when swimming there.

There are two coastlines to Lannacombe! There is the low line of

The coastline between Beesands and Hallsands

cliffs which we followed, and a little inland is another line of much higher cliffs, a coastline from the distant past when sea levels were higher. Our stop at Lannacombe was brief, as the stench from a sewage outlet made it an unpleasant place to eat lunch.

We thought that it would be a welcome change to return to Beesands via the maze of narrow lanes, which seem to go nowhere in particular but follow the deep combes. Our selected route led us up through Kellaton, to the former school at Huckham which now acts as a fieldwork/residential centre for Exmouth School, the biggest comprehensive in this country (and noted so in the Guinness Book

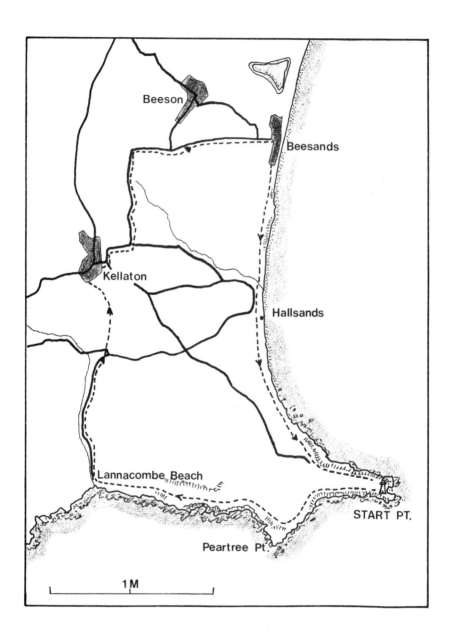

Beeson

Beesands

Kellaton

Hallsands

Lannacombe Beach

Peartree Pt.

START PT.

1 M

90

of Records). From this, the centre of the rural universe, we headed back to the coast at Beesands.

Dame Fortune, in the shape of Cyril, Landlord of the Cricket Inn, smiled on us as he opened the pub's doors the moment we arrived. Even then, two locals managed to beat us through the door, proving the theory that the air at Beesands is highly conducive to a good thirst. Cyril showed us his large collection of photographs, depicting the storms which have hit this coastline in recent years. Also, around the walls of the inn are many pictures of old Hallsands, and many enormous crabs (dead). This was a splendid walk of great interest.

15
DevonAir Sponsored Walk—Exeter to Torquay

For some strange reason, just because I write books about walking, describe walks on the radio and give illustrated talks about walking to interested groups, people seem to think I actually enjoy walking! So there I was, having a quiet drink in a local pub, when David Cousins, Managing Director of DevonAir Radio, casually suggested that I lead a sponsored walk in aid of the DevonAir Devon Care Special Appeal.

Once committed, I duly consulted my map and discovered that it takes 28 miles of countryside lanes and paths to travel between the two studios at Exeter and Torquay. A more direct route was possible, along the main roads, but it seemed a wiser move to follow the backroads, as they would have far less traffic, and therefore be a safer corridor, through the Devon air to Torquay.

When the idea was mooted, my initial reaction was that we would probably only attract a handful of participants. After all, it is a longer-than-marathon distance and hardened walkers would normally shun the combined evils of metalled highways and sponsored walks.

Stephen Ayres, presenter extraordinaire, spent many hours arranging details like first aid, insurance, police liaison and 'sweeping up' the possible dropouts. Meanwhile, I planned the route and photocopied the 1929 Ordnance Survey Map of the area, using such an archaic oracle so as not to infringe copyright. Naturally minor details, such as motorways and the occasional main road,

were missing but at least it did show both Exeter and Torquay! And I did pencil in a dotted line, which unfortunately was rather faint, between the two towns on the map.

And so it was, the day dawned (but only just), with heavy overcast skies making the November light extremely dull.

Within the St David's Hill studios, there was great activity. The sponsored walk was only part of a much larger campaign to raise money for deserving local charities, an 'on-air auction' being the major attraction. In reception hordes of walkers were huddled to sign on for, what was to become, more of a voyage than a walk through the Devonshire countryside.

Amazingly, we had 54 game persons keen to attempt this hike. It was too many for a single group, so we split the pilgrims into four units, with presenters John Brocks and David Fitzgerald accounting for two of them, whilst Dennis Johnston MBE (and mountaineer) led a third unit. Yours truly agreed to take the remnants, an assortment of stragglers from all walks of life, temporarily united for a single walk.

The restrictive hours of daylight in November dictated that a pace in excess of 4 miles an hour was necessary if the outskirts of Torquay were going to be reached before nightfall, that is about 4.30 pm.

We set off across the windswept Iron Bridge in Exeter, in the direction of the level towpath of the Exeter Canal to Countess Weir. As so often happens on events like this, each group consisted of fast, medium and slow strollers. This meant that there was soon an intermingling of the four tribes.

To maintain the interest of the listening public, it had been agreed that I should 'ring in' our progress at every telephone box.

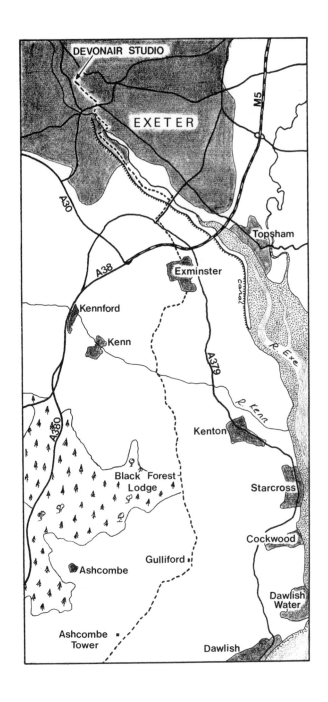

However, the route only passed a few, and my first attempt at Exminster was fraught with difficulties.

As the whole weekend was devoted to charity, an army of volunteer helpers had been brought in, and some of these manned the phones, which were obviously very busy. When I eventually managed to get through to tell my tale, I was greeted with the phrase, "What sponsored walk?"

I trusted to luck that a message would get through as, during the precious minutes spent fumbling with coins, struggling with bulky rucksacks in confined spaces and conducting confused conversations, the procession of participants marched past the telephone kiosk and kept on going—beyond the junction where they should have forked off!

Frantically waving my arms to attract attention, I shouted in their wake. As luck would have it, my cry of desperation must have been borne on the wind for, within minutes, my flock reappeared looking suitably sheepish!

At the bottom of Exminster Hill, in a howling gale, I carefully explained to them that, if they knew the way ahead and could confidently interpret the map, then they were welcome to go ahead. But if they had any doubt as to the prescribed route, then they should stick with me.

Now, I had been somewhat surprised that they had missed the first turning, but I was rendered speechless, less than 400 yards later, when a whole horde of the adventurers doggedly strayed from the path yet again.

This time it was out of the question to sprint after them, for it would have turned my 28 miles into a very much longer romp. As it later transpired, at the post mortem, some of the "strays" had made a bold attempt to cut across country to regain the right route. They had a circular tour of a large wood, complete with dense undergrowth and a badger sett full of awkwardly located holes. In addition to this they scaled high banks, and foraged their way through all manner of obstacles, only to complete this detour by ending up at the point where they started!

Leading this clandestine breakaway group was John Brocks, who had, reluctantly, been 'badgered' into the walk.

Meanwhile, back on the correct route, the participants entered a section of gentle road walking which took us past Haydon Common and on towards Black Forest Lodge, near Mamhead. Our path followed an ancient trade route, which originally linked up with river crossings at Topsham.

As a precaution, I chalked an arrow on the ground at every crossroads to indicate the correct way to go. It is surprising how quickly a stick of chalk wears away when trying to draw an arrow on a wet, bumpy road.

All went exceedingly well until we arrived at Gulliford. Beyond the steep hill, above this hamlet, a mighty chasm appeared before us—the valley of Dawlish Water. Innocently the throng sauntered down to cross this delightful watercourse, in order to essay the climb towards Ashcombe Tower.

The next mile and a half, a continuous and often steep ascent, brought gasps of astonishment as well as breathlessness. Our prolonged rise to the relative Alpine Heights of Little Haldon wore many of the walkers out. Notwithstanding this, the elements showed no pity, and contrived to produce thick hill mist and cool, penetrating rain.

However, we didn't feel so hard done by when we chanced upon a fellow mortal who had landed in a predicament worse than our own. The heavy rains had created an enormous puddle, many inches deep and many yards long. An unfortunate motorist had stalled his car in the deluge and had "flooded" his engine in a bid to restart it. There

really was very little we could do to help the poor man, as the water around his vehicle was prohibitively deep for walkers doomed to spend several more hours struggling onward. At least when I went back a few weeks later, he was no longer there! Presumably he had reached a phone box and called out an AA or RAC submarine to rescue him.

Vehicles, with headlights ablaze, loomed out of the mist, their occupants no doubt startled to witness our sodden procession through the gloom. There were no golfers out on Teignmouth Golf Course, as we skirted the greens to enter the back lane down towards Teignmouth. Just as we had entered the fog at about 600 feet A.S.L., we correspondingly left the fog at the same level on our descent.

By now we had crossed many junctions and I was on my third, and final, stick of chalk. This was now so small that on the last countryside junction above Teignmouth, I almost took the skin off my fingertips, trying to make an identifiable direction arrow. I hoped that the lunch time inn would be able to provide a refill, but that was still a good mile ahead.

I very much doubt whether the next landmark would be believed, had I not included photographic evidence of its existence. Teignmouth's very own Statue of Liberty stood in the garden of a very ordinary looking suburban house. I hope I wasn't taking a liberty by snapping a few pictures of it.

By comparison, the late lunch time break at The Talbot in Teignmouth was quite a dull experience to relate, so I shan't.

The journey over Shaldon Bridge was an uncomfortable one, as great gusts of wind made walking a straight course almost impossible. At the end of the bridge, a few minutes chat was exchanged with the St John Ambulance team, who had done such a good job

The young lady in the capable hands of the St John Ambulance team is a taxi driver from Brixham. She completed the 28 mile walk and raised more money than anyone else!

monitoring the progress and welfare of the walkers.

Despite the deluge, one or two of Ringmore's residents were in their doorways to wish us good luck and cheer us on. Moral support of that type was particularly beneficial as the climb out of this estuary settlement, and over the hill to Stokeinteignhead, was another arduous one.

It was now about 3.30 pm and it was far too dull to take any photographs. The sticks of chalk acquired at the Talbot had also eroded to nothingness, and the directional arrows could hardly be seen by now anyway. Nobody could possibly tell which way the Indians went!

The countryside between Stokeinteignhead and the edge of Torquay at Great Hill, is exceedingly hilly with deep, sheltered combes between each lofty hillock. Consequently, in the fast fading light we followed a muddy lane, with bottomless puddles that produced many sudden shrieks. This took us across the top of one of these hills, only to plunge down into the deep ravine of Higher Rocombe Barton. Beyond lay an enormous hill, called appropriately Great Hill, which saw us into the relative civilisation of outer Torquay.

There were no cheering crowds thronging the streets to welcome us to journey's end; only the wind blowing and the rain pouring down with relentless fury.

The last three miles were virtually all downhill, but there was only

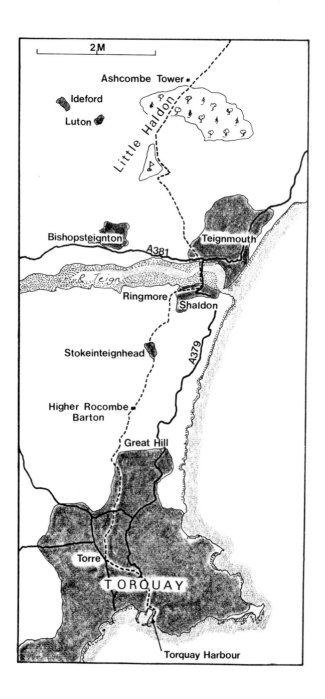

98

about half an hour left in which to fit a live broadcast in order to retell the tale. Young Darren Marsh, a former Exeter Harrier, had been my constant companion on this stroll. He agreed to pace me as we ran and fast walked those last three miles, which we covered in about 25 minutes. Considering the state of dress, the encumbrances of rucksacks and other equipment, and the sheer bloodymindedness of the elements, it wasn't at all bad going.

Thoroughly soaked, completely exhausted, but very happy, we entered the Torquay studio on a wave of euphoria. There was such a joyful welcome in store for us that it made the memory of the labours and tribulations disappear in an instant. We had made it by 4.45 pm and a quick burst of spontaneous broadcasting completed a memorable day. Out of the 54 magnificent participants, 47 completed the walk—the remaining seven fell just short of the target. The amount raised was £1,700 which went to local charities.

16

In The Land of Tamar and Tavy

There is an almost self contained kingdom, in the very far west of Devon, abutting the River Tamar, which is often ignored by the multitudes of visitors each summer. The word "kingdom" is indeed appropriate, as the Bere Peninsula extends southwards from a narrow neck of land between the Rivers Tamar and Tavy. To the south it opens out for several miles, before tapering again to a point where the two rivers finally agree to join forces.

The Bere peninsula is rich in mineral deposits and, at one time, the streets of its capital, Bere Alston, were thronged with miners. More recently, almost the whole peninsula was covered by cherry orchards, a sight which must have gladdened the eye and truly exploited the sense of smell.

The main reason for the apparent low number of visitors must surely lie with its relative inaccessibility by road. It is necessary to make the Bere Peninsula a positive destination, as roads along it lead to nowhere in particular. The two road routes to the 'island' come from the A390 to the north, and from across the diminutive Denham Bridge, straddling the Tavy, on the eastern frontier.

Perhaps one of the best ways to reach this small princeless principality is via the Tamar Valley Branch Line, which plies its way northwards from Plymouth. To see the two carriage train today, it is hard to imagine the freight carried along the line in the past. Early this century it was commonplace for a dozen or more wagon loads of flowers to leave the Tamar Valley, each day, along this iron railroad. In the summer of 1908, no less than 100 tons of straw-berries were transported to an eager and vast hinterland. In the inter-war years the railway carried 15,000 passengers a year, but it should be noted that the line then continued on through Tavistock and beyond to Exeter. In the grim years of the Second World War it enabled the masses to leave Plymouth and head for the relative safety of the hills. It is on record that every available bed space in the Bere Peninsula was occupied. This included hen houses, barns and garden sheds!

But we must not get side tracked, and as our walking quartet all thought along similar lines, we took the train out from Plymouth. Puns about railways abounded. Someone asked, "Was the Bere Peninsula a buffer state?" because it was wedged between the two mighty opposing powers of Devon and Cornwall. The response was quite cutting! We stationed ourselves at various corners of the loco-motive, and applied our trained minds to good use until we finally ran out of steam. It was obviously just the ticket needed to signal the beginning of another ramble. Thus, at Bere Ferrers, we alighted

Bere Ferrers, where Tavy joins Tamar

100

from the train and promptly began our exploration of this new territory.

Bere Ferrers is an extremely small settlement which runs down to the shores of the River Tavy. The church, the pub and the post office jostle for the closest maritime location. The first part of this place name has various translations: it means a fortified place, a wooded location or even a peninsular. The Ferrers part of the name derives from a French Norman family, and means that it has a 'Smithy' connection, presumably the sort that shoe horses.

The waterfront scene which presented itself to us must be one of the finest, most unspoilt views in Devon. We saw no cars, and passed no people, as we headed north eastwards to Gnatham, itself on its own small peninsular. The two wooded valleys of the Tavy and its tributary looked inviting and, had it been windy, would have afforded a pleasant sheltered walk. However it was the sort of day when the freshness of upland air was appreciated.

Such philosophy resulted in a route past Collytown and on to Bere Alston, a strangely independent looking former mining settlement. It would be wrong to give an opinion about this large village, or small town, on the evidence of a swift safari through its streets. Somehow the character of the place was not typically Devon, nor remotely Cornish. I had no idea of what to expect and now that I have been there, I can't make up my mind whether I like it or not. That is the beauty of being decisive! Perhaps if they buy my books in great numbers, it might swing my opinion . . . It is unquestionably an individualistic place.

The most exciting railway journey in South West England must be between Bere Alston and Gunnislake. The line swiftly plunges to cross the magnificent viaduct at Calstock, a typically Cornish place, before sinuously contouring the great spur above Morwellham, on its ever climbing ascendency, through market gardens and disused mine workings, on its way up to Gunnislake. The others were almost persuaded to give this journey a try, as an extension to the walk, but the one and a half hour long wait at this remote station was less attractive.

Therefore we descended past Bere Alston station to reach the Tamar at a point shown as Buttspill on the map. In minutes we were opposite Calstock, and duly impressed by this lively riverside port. Curiously, in the last century it gained a notorious reputation for

Calstock

heavy drinking, and also for an evil smell. It appears that out of the
population of 2,500, more than two thirds were without water
closets, and the streets were ankle deep in filth. In addition to these
delights, it appears that refuse from pig sties was heaped against
houses, as were the remains of undrained refuse from a slaughter-
house. Fortunately for visitors, the waterside tea rooms were
relatively unaffected and passengers alighting from the steamers
could hire donkeys, at stable prices, to escape from Calstock if
necessary.

By the time all the Tamar tales had been told, we had contoured
the bend of the river and passed the lovely Cotehele Quay on the
opposite bank. The path was followed with due care and attention to
Hewton. At this point the river viciously backtracks on itself,
flowing first south westwards and then north eastwards, before
resuming a southerly course towards Devonport and the open sea.

Now that the puns had been put away in favour of serious conversation, our dialogue examined the history of this glorious river, and our attention turned to the thousands of people who must have been conveyed along the Tamar. Perhaps the multitudes were encouraged to voyage up this river because of the example set by Queen Victoria in 1856, when she steamed (or rather the boat did!) up river to visit the Duke of Bedford at Endsleigh.

Only four years later, steamers like the good ship *Fairy* carried passengers who hungrily anticipated a feast at Mr Jackson's tea and fruit gardens at Bere Ferrers, where a large marquee was added for those who wanted to dance. Things were less dignified by the 1890s when, so many steam ships plied the river vying for trade that, "bumping" in mid stream became a common and dangerous

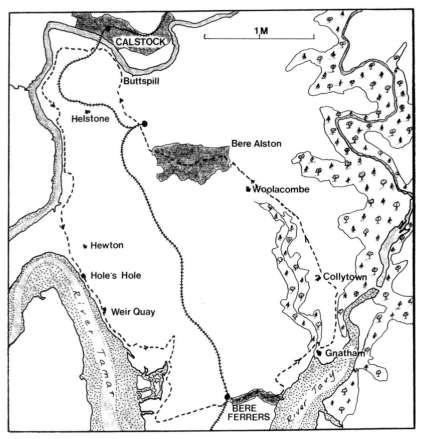

practice. Even so, most of the 100,000 trippers each year survived to attend dances on the quays at places like Morwellham and Weir Head.

As we were tied to the train times our progress, beyond the curious sounding Hole's Hole, along the flats of Weir Quay and back over the hills to Bere Ferrers, was route marching at its best. We only paused once to gaze longingly at Cargreen on the opposite side of the river. We'd had a good day out and it was a real bonus to sit behind the engine driver and spectate, like small boys on the front seat of a bus, Brunel's great bridge at Saltash, the giant dockyards of Devonport and the urban ugliness of Plymouth. At least Plymothians are lucky to have these islands on their doorstep on which to get marooned whenever they desire escape.

17
If You go down to Fernworthy Forest
You'll be sure of a Big Surprise!

'Magnificent' was the only word to describe them! In their gleaming, red livery, Devon General Buses provided a bus service from Exeter to Chagford which defied any suitable narrative. Nobody else could have created such an unusual way of weaving across the Dartmoor borderland, to reach the moorland fringe at Chagford. This straight line distance of about 16 miles was extended to nearer 30, in order to explore the ups and downs of the Teign Valley, the ins and outs of villages, like Dunsford and, of course, the initial guided tour of Exeter which reached the parts other buses failed to reach.

In our youth, we frequently made this epic journey which occupied almost two hours of our life, and left us the remainder to recover. The only compensation for us was that the PAYE driver accepted that were were all under fourteen. Well, we were still at school!

That August morning, Chagford was alive with people. Smart ladies sporting expensive tweed accompanied by their husbands

Peering down on Chagford from Meldon Hill. Castle Drogo can be spied in the top right

wearing deer stalkers and plus fours, were visible proof of the town's wealth. Being impressionable youngsters we deliberately passed close enough to catch the tones of their voices, which echoed with strains of dinner parties, hunting, fly fishing and trips 'up to town'. This was far removed from some of our choice language imbibed on the long, hard road walk from Chagford towards the moor at Fernworthy. This was attributable to the thick mist encountered as we got above a thousand feet at Frenchbeer. It effectively ruled out our intended journey to Cranmere Pool, not because of our inability to find it using a compass, but there seemed little point in visiting such a fog bound wilderness just for the sake of it.

The three miles road walk out from Chagford did seem like a route march. We didn't even have the compensation of a scenic view, as the visibility was down to some thirty yards. Fernworthy Reservoir, which could be heard but not seen, was started in 1936 but not finished until 1942. A major setback occurred, in early August 1938, when a freak thunderstorm, of great ferocity, forced several million gallons of water and mud hurtling down the South Teign river to destroy much of the early work on the dam. As this is termed "An Act of God", He certainly must have been in a parti-cularly grumpy mood! The reservoir contains some 380 million gallons of water and is nearly 70 feet deep in the middle. In drought years the waters recede sufficiently for Fernworthy Bridge, and a small clapper, to be seen closely. The water is piped to Tottiford, Trenchford and Kennick Reservoirs, on the high ridge of land between the Wrey and the Middle Teign Valleys. From here it is dis-tributed so that Torquinians can consume it before redistributing it themselves.

The dull proceedings got a much needed boost at the end of the No Through Road around Fernworthy reservoir. A mini-van was parked just off the road and caught our attention by the way it creaked and vibrated rhythmically, with no apparent persons visible in the front seat. Innocent youths that we were, we were quite offended by the language of the angry face at the steamed up window, telling us in no uncertain terms to clear off. Realising his state of undress would hamper a chase, we ambled off into the woods at a leisurely pace.

These distracting events evidently caused our map reading to

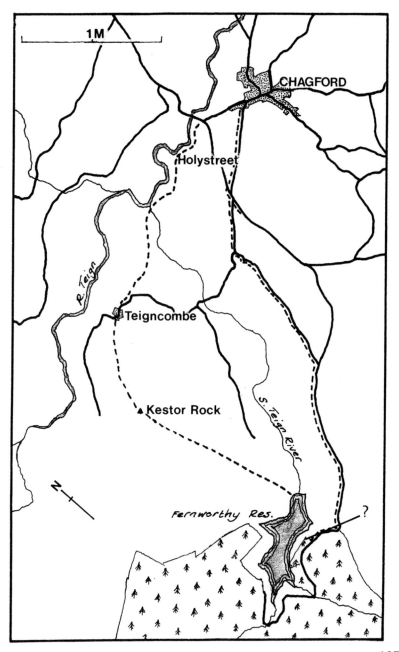

CHAGFORD

Holystreet

R. Teign

Teigncombe

▲ Kestor Rock

S. Teign River

N

Fernworthy Res.

?

1M

suffer for, after a while of floundering around in Fernworthy forest, we had to admit that we were unaware of our exact location. He who bore the map and compass bore the brunt of the blame—poor old Willy.

There is usually an optimist in every gang of misguided adventurers, and in this case it was Clive who clearly recognised some of the trees and was convinced that, out of the millions of conifers in Fernworthy, the ones ahead of us were those which lined the avenue to our intended destination of Teignhead Farm. This though was not the case as, back at the reservoir we emerged at the exact same spot.

With a quick bang on the roof of the minivan, we quickly ran away at breakneck speed to follow the edge of the reservoir towards Thornworthy Tor although, with the dense vegetation and further poor map reading, got to see neither of these spots.

Before the reservoir was constructed, Fernworthy was regarded as a village but this is a misleading description for it simply consisted of three, closely sited hill farms. Fernworthy Farm was located but a stone's throw from where the courting couple had parked. However, its ruins lie not beneath the waters of the reservoir, for no buildings were drowned at Fernworthy, but under dense undergrowth and trees beside the present road. In 1840 the farm was owned by Sir Humphrey Davie, presumably not the one who invented the safety lamp for miners, or laughing gas for anaesthetists, for he died in 1829. Where the great forest stands is an area which once yielded corn, probably of an inferior quality. Also concealed in this densely afforested area are the prehistoric remains of many hut circles and stone rows.

Perhaps it was a case of us not seeing the wood for the trees, for we had to concede that it was just one of those days when the open northern moors didn't want to know us. We skirted the edge of the reservoir in the direction of Thornworthy Tor, crossed a small tributary of the South Teign, and headed gamely onwards into the thick, damp, clinging mists.

In a Dartmoor fog, all known objects seem to take on a different and oft-times eerie appearance. On this occasion, Kestor Rock looked like a mountain range, as it loomed from nowhere out of the mist. Because the conditions had become so unpleasant for walking, an alternative destination was sought. Unanimously the group assented to it being the Buller's Arms in Chagford. And so our group of 5 strapping 16-year-olds made light of the track and road through Holystreet Manor to reach Chagford in record time.

There followed a theme of 'halves' in the next hour or so. We consumed several halves of ale, waited half an hour for the bus, and half expected to be charged full fare. But despite breathing our beery breath over the driver, we still managed to travel halves on the bus back to Exeter!

The first ever country bus service in Devon ran out to Chagford . . . and it's due in any moment now!

OTHER OBELISK PUBLICATIONS

THE TORBAY BOOK   Chips Barber

Did you hear about the smuggler who went to his own funeral? Or about the ghost who threw Beverley Nichols out of a window? Did you know that the toilets at Paignton Harbour were once a coastguard station or the ones on Torquay sea front were once an old toll house? Perhaps you may have been fooled by television and film makers who have used Torbay as the Mediterranean! The Torbay Book is packed with a vast number of strange tales and surprises from an area which includes Maidencombe, Babbacombe, St Marychurch, Torquay, Cockington, Paignton, Goodrington and Brixham.

AROUND & ABOUT THE HALDON HILLS   Chips Barber

The Haldon Hills lie between the Exe Valley and Dartmoor. This books deals with almost every aspect of this 12 miles long hill range including geology, quarrying, railways, roads, walking, wildlife and legends. There are also detailed studies of the towns and villages in and around these hills.

THE LOST CITY OF EXETER   Chips Barber

If you enjoy unusual anecdotes and would like to know the real Exeter—the villages within and without—its entertainment past and present, its sporting prowess and much more, you will love this lively book. It contains many illustrations including aerial views of the city.

IDE   Bill Rowland

This is the first book of our village series and is a colourful portrayal of life in a country village near Exeter from the turn of the century to the present day. It includes many entertaining and humorous anecdotes and gives a very good insight into the social conditions which prevailed in such an environment.

ADVENTURE THROUGH RED DEVON   Raymond B Cattell

This is probably the finest book ever written about the coastline, estuaries and rivers of South and East Devon. It is a warm, personal, and humorous account of journeys made through these areas between 1931 and 1935. There are detailed accounts of the history and unusual stories of all the places passed during these adventures. Ray Cattell gets marooned in Torbay, shipwrecked at Lyme Regis, encounters vicious swans, wicked weirs and obstinate locals on his voyage up the River Exe and spent a summer on a very different Dawlish Warren as it was in the 1930s. The "joys" of Newton Abbot station, the Teign's tidal race and beautiful girls all play their part in this book.

UNDER SAIL THROUGH SOUTH DEVON AND DARTMOOR

Raymond B Cattell

This is a continuation of "Red Devon". The windswept, rocky landscape of Dartmoor and the wild, unspoilt coastline of South Devon are the two areas explored in this book. Raymond Cattell has adventures along the coastline, up the rivers and estuaries and across the moorland hills. Entertaining and informative it will raise many smiles and perhaps even a few eyebrows as he encounters nude bathers at Dartington, has a race to Cranmere Pool, meets a Princetown Pixie, stumbles across a long lost port on the Tamar, is nearly blown up at Berry Head and scorched at Prawle Point. If you have the spirit of adventure and a good sense of fun you will be thrilled and enthralled by this great Devonshire safari.

AN EXETER BOYHOOD   Frank Retter

These tales are about childhood memories in Exeter. Frank tells of school life, markets, scouting adventures to green fields long gone, hardship and poverty. Illustrated by old and new photographs, and line drawings, it is a fascinating study of life at the turn of the century.

AN EAST DEVON FARM AND ITS VILLAGE   Frank Retter

Frank Retter has spent several years tracing his own family's history back through many generations. His family's story takes place in East Devon with the backcloth of the Ottery St Mary, Exmouth and Clyst Honiton areas prominently featured. It is the last location to which Frank devotes much of the text of this book and he gives a revealing glimpse into country life in East Devon in the past.

THE GREAT WALKS OF DARTMOOR   Terry Bound

This is the first book to include all the recognised long walks which take place on Dartmoor. It includes the Abbots Way, the North/South crossing, the Lich Way, the OATS walks, the Perambulation, the Dartmoor 100, the Ten Tors, the Mariners Way and the Tom Cobley walk. These walks are sufficiently detailed to enable the fit enthusiast to follow them.

RAMBLING IN THE PLYMOUTH COUNTRYSIDE

Dave Woolley and Martin Lister

With Dartmoor on the doorstep it is very easy to overlook the wonderful borderland, valley and coastal scenery which fringe the high moors. Dave Woolley and Martin Lister have combined forces to explore some splendid scenery in and around Plymouth. The book is extremely well illustrated and contains a large number of interesting and entertaining tales from the Tamar to the Yealm, along the coast, up the creeks and across the many windswept commons and downs around Plymouth.

DIARY OF A DARTMOOR WALKER   Chips Barber

If you have enjoyed "Devonshire Walker" you will find "Dartmoor Walker" an excellent companion to it. For a similarly modest investment you can treat yourself to another 21 moorland adventures—from the comfort of your own fireside chair (or park bench depending on your financial circumstances!)—with the added bonus of an entire chapter on Dartmoor Letterboxes. This is an ideal book for the person with a sense of humour.

★   ★   ★   ★   ★

Illustrated Talks

Chips Barber spends a lot of time giving lively talks about the books he has written. If your group or organisation would like an entertaining, informative and fully illustrated talk, please contact Obelisk Publications for further details and bookings.

All these books are readily available from Obelisk Publications, 2 Church Hill, Pinhoe, Exeter. Telephone (0392) 68556.